EXETER MEDIEVAL TEXTS AND STUDIES
General Editors: Marion Glasscoe, M.J. Swanton and Vincent Gillespie

T0341419

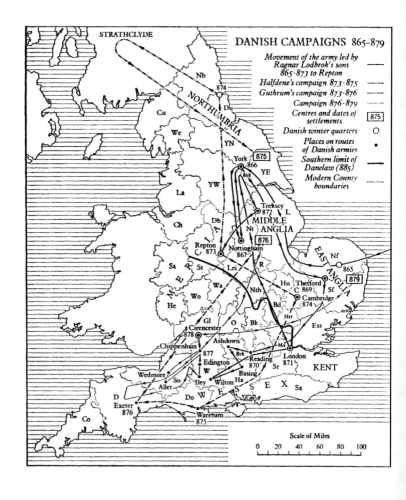

DANISH CAMPAIGNS 865-879

Movement of the army led by Ragnar Lodbrok's sons 865-873 to Repton ——————

Halfdene's campaign 873-875 ——————

Guthrum's campaign 873-876 - - - - - -

Campaign 876-879 -·-·-·-·-

Centres and dates of settlements 875

Danish winter quarters ○

Places on routes of Danish armies •

Southern limit of Danelaw (885) ▬▬▬▬

Modern County boundaries

STRATHCLYDE

Nb

NORTHUMBRIA
874
Du

Cu

We

YN

York 875
866
868
YE

La

YW

Ch

Db
MIDDLE
Torksey ANGLIA
872 L
Nt
876
Repton Nottingham
873 867
Lei R EAST
Sa St ANGLIA
Nf
Wa Nth Hu 865
Thetford 879
Wo C 869 Sf
He Bd Cambridge
874
Gl Ess
Cirencester O Bk
878
Chippenham Ashdown Ms
877 Brk London
Edington Reading 871
W Basing KENT
Wedmore So St
Iley Wilton Ha
Aller E S S E X Sx
Do W Do
D
Exeter Co
876
Wareham
875

Scale of Miles
0 20 40 60 80 100

THE PARKER CHRONICLE

CHRONICLE

832-900

Edited by

A. H. SMITH

with a bibliography compiled by

M. J. Swanton

UNIVERSITY
of
EXETER
PRESS

First published in Methuen's Old
English Library, London, 1935

This revised edition, University of Exeter 1980

University of Exeter Press
Reed Hall, Streatham Drive
Exeter, EX4 4QR
UK

www.exeterpress.co.uk

Printed digitally since 2006

© Estate of A.H. Smith

ISBN 978 0 85989 099 1

Printed and bound by CPI Group (UK) Ltd, Croydon, CR0 4YY

PREFACE

THE object of this edition is to present a reliable text of a section of the oldest manuscript of the Chronicle. A complete section such as this will give a much clearer picture of the structure of the Chronicle than isolated and disconnected selections. It is true that in this way some interesting passages (such as the Cynewulf-Cyneheard episode) are omitted, but the possibility of a reasonable estimate of the historical value of the Chronicle and the possibility of a fair appraisement of its literary qualities are important gains. The particular portion printed here covers the earliest Danish invasions and Ælfred's reign and is the work of several almost contemporary scribes. The scope of the edition is limited by the amount of original text, for many of the major problems involve a study of all manuscripts of the Chronicles. Some effort has been made, however, to indicate in the introduction and notes what these problems are. The constant reference to the works of Mawer, Beaven, Stenton and above all of Plummer will shew to what extent I, like all other students of the Chronicles, am indebted to these scholars. I am indebted to Sir Edwyn Hoskyns, Bt., Librarian of Corpus Christi College, Cambridge, for allowing me access to the manuscript, and my thanks are due to Professor Bruce Dickins for some valuable suggestions and for reading the proofs, as well as to Professor R. W. Chambers and Professor E. V. Gordon.

A. H. SMITH

PREFACE TO THIS EDITION

THIS edition incorporates revisions made by the late A. H. Smith prior to his death in 1967. In addition the bibliography has been recast and brought up to date.

M.J.S.

CONTENTS

ABBREVIATIONS

Beaven	.	.	M. L. R. Beaven, EHR xxxiii. 328–42 (1918)
BT	.	.	J. Bosworth and T. N. Toller, *An Anglo-Saxon Dictionary*, 1882, 1921
EETS	.	.	Early English Text Society (Original Series)
EHR	.	.	English Historical Review
EPN	.	.	English Place-Name Society publications
ESt	.	.	Englische Studien
Hoffmann-Hirtz		.	M. Hoffmann-Hirtz, *Une Chronique Anglo-Saxonne*, 1933
Mawer	.	.	A. Mawer, *Palaestra* cxlvii (1925)
ME	.	.	Middle English
MLN	.	.	Modern Language Notes
NED	.	.	New English Dictionary
ODan	.	.	Old Danish
OE	.	.	Old English
OET	.	.	H. Sweet, *Oldest English Texts*, 1885
OIcel	.	.	Old Icelandic
ON	.	.	Old Norse
Plummer	.	.	C. Plummer, *Two of the Saxon Chronicles Parallel*, 1892–9
Stevenson	.	.	W. H. Stevenson, *Asser's Life of Alfred*, 1904
Thorpe	.	.	B. Thorpe, *The Anglo-Saxon Chronicle*, 1861
WSax .	.	.	West Saxon

THE
PARKER CHRONICLE

INTRODUCTION

THE ultimate origin of the type of historical composition represented by the Old English Chronicles is probably to be sought in the Easter Tables * which were drawn up to assist the clergy to determine the date of this great Christian festival in any year in an era. The tables were generally arranged with the year of the era and the figures for determining the date of Easter on a single line, and with their ample margins they provided a suitable framework into which short historical notices could be fitted, not as the basis of a contemporary history, but to distinguish the years from one another as they receded and grew confused in memory. Moreover, the Easter Tables required and gave rise to an era or system of reckoning by years which was also necessary before anything in the way of historical annals could be attempted.†

The difference between the primitive type of annal, which was nothing more than a short notice opposite the

* This problem is considered by R. L. Poole, *Chronicles and Annals* (Oxford 1926). See also Plummer II. cxiv.

† On the general problem of the development of the Christian era out of the cycle of years invented by Dionysus Exiguus in 525 as the basis of an Easter Table, see R. L. Poole, *Medieval Reckonings of Time* (1921), 39 ff. Dionysus uses one of the dates computed as the year of Christ's birth as a starting-point for a series of years to accompany his Easter Table. This series of years was first used as an era in England in the late seventh century and largely through the popularity of Bede's work it became the recognized system.

year-number in an Easter Table, and the Old English Chronicles is largely one of intention. The Chronicles aim at being repositories of facts grouped together in years. They are long past the stage of the single-line entry, but the first scribe of the Parker MS was still influenced by these primitive annals when he wrote a series of year-numbers on successive lines on the assumption that a single line would suffice for each year—only to find that he needed two or more. This explains why some of the annals are opposite several year-numbers.[*]

In the Chronicle facts are related impersonally, excepting, perhaps, the outburst in 896, *Næfde se here, ʒodes þonces, Anʒelcyn ealles forspiðe ʒebrocod.* And similarly apart from one or two references to preceding annals, as for example the repeated allusions to the date the great Danish army came into this country,[†] there is no attempt to relate these facts to one another or to inquire into their causes. The material is uneven, sometimes an important fact is missing, and, as will be seen below (pp. 9 ff), the chronology itself is occasionally uncertain. In spite of these defects the Old English Chronicles remain the most fruitful source for the history of England between Bede and the Norman Conquest. Besides this, the fact that they are vernacular compositions and, in the later years, at all events, not based upon Latin writings, gives them additional value, for in them we have the best examples of early Old English prose. Occasionally the style is clumsy and ambiguous (cf, for example, 837[5], 871[25], 871[39], 893[8]), but usually the meaning is clearly and definitely expressed and there is some variety in the mode of expression (cf below, p. 14).

Versions and Origin of the Chronicle

There are seven extant manuscripts of the Chronicles, falling, as Plummer shews, into four distinct groups [‡] :

[*] Cf textual notes to 833, 840, 860, below.
[†] Cf 893[1], 893[99], 894[16], 895[1], 895[22], &c, also 892[1].
[‡] Plummer II. xxiii ff.

I. MS A[1] (the Parker MS), formerly Archbishop Parker's, now Corpus Christi College, Cambridge, MS 173, folios 1–32, followed by the Acts of Lanfranc, the Laws of Ine and Ælfred, &c. The text of the present edition is derived from this MS. For the years covered by the present text the following hands may be noted. The first hand continues to the foot of fol. 16a (see notes p. 40) ; the second hand starts on fol. 16b and, according to Thorpe I. 162 and Plummer I. 85n, II. xxv, finishes at the bottom of this fol. 16b in the middle of a sentence which is carried on by the third hand on fol. 17a * ; the third hand finishes at the bottom of fol. 17b. The fourth hand starts on fol. 18a and this is the last hand until after 900. The first scribe may well have completed his section about the year 891, and there is nothing in the character of the remaining hands to shew that they do not belong approximately to the period covered by their particular entries, though on purely palaeographical grounds they might belong to any period in the tenth century. Besides the main hands, there are interpolations by later scribes, and where these can be definitely ascribed to later hands they are printed in italics in the present edition. Whatever the origin of the manuscript (see below, p. 8), it was

* It is not certain from the general character or details of penmanship that the ' second ' and ' third ' hands of Plummer's list (II. xxv), followed by M. R. James, *A Descriptive Catalogue of the MSS in Corpus Christi College, Cambridge*, 1912, I. 396, are to be considered different. The only difference is that the second scribe was cramming matter on fol. 16b ; fol. 16, it should be noted, is the last folio of the second gathering (cf Plummer II. xxiv, M. R. James, *op. cit.* I. 395). When the second scribe took up the MS he would have only one page to fill up at the end of the original MS ; he may, not unnaturally, have crammed matter on this page and he certainly followed the punctures made by the first scribe on fol. 16a as guide marks for the disposition of his lines, for the lines on fol. 16b coincide exactly with those on fol. 16a. But this scribe would have felt disposed to more spacious writing in his new gathering on fol. 17a, as his ascenders and descenders have more length than those of the original scribe of the Parker MS. It may be added that the MS is now so tightly bound and the head- and tailbands fit so closely that it is not possible to check the collation.

certainly kept at Winchester in the tenth century, for entries with a particular Winchester interest are confined to the tenth century (see Plummer II. xcv). In the eleventh century this manuscript was transferred to Canterbury where many of the Kentish interpolations were made (as 870[6], 890[9]).

MS A[2], British Museum, Cotton MS Otho B XI, which was almost completely destroyed in the fire of 1731 ; Wheloc based his edition of the Chronicle on this manuscript, and the extant remains have been printed by K. Horst in ESt xxii. 447–450, xxv. 195. Recently a sixteenth-century transcript of the complete manuscript has come into the possession of the British Museum (Add. MS 43703), an account of which will appear in Dr. R. Flower's edition in this series of an hitherto unpublished Old English poem on Fasting. MS A[2] was a transcript of A[1] probably made at Winchester in the eleventh century, though M. Kupferschmidt on rather slender grounds attempts to make out a more elaborate relationship (ESt xiii. 165–187).

II. A lost chronicle similar to A[1], sent possibly to Abingdon, where some of the official continuations and a Mercian Register were incorporated :

MS B, British Museum, Cotton MS Tiberius A VI, is a copy of this chronicle made about 1000 and subsequently kept at Canterbury but without additions ;

MS C, British Museum, Cotton MS Tiberius B I, is a mid-eleventh century copy of the lost Abingdon chronicle which had been kept up to date ; MS C was itself kept up to 1066.

III. A copy of the original chronicle sent to the North was expanded by materials from Bede and other early northern sources, and it was kept up with additional northern material and the official continuations :

MS D, British Museum, Cotton MS Tiberius B IV, is a mid-eleventh century transcript of a copy of this northern chronicle which had been sent to the Worcester diocese ; MS D was then continued to 1079.

IV. A chronicle which was akin to the northern ancestor of MS D but which did not incorporate all the West Saxon continuations was compiled and sent to Canterbury where it was kept till after the Conquest :

MS E (the ' Laud manuscript '), Bodleian MS, Laud 636, was a transcript of this Canterbury chronicle made at Peterborough about 1122 and there continued independently till 1154 ;

MS F, British Museum, Cotton MS Domitian A VIII, is a bilingual (English and Latin) epitome of this same Canterbury chronicle, made at Canterbury after the Conquest.*

The growth of these four groups of Chronicles may be shortly stated in this way : in the ninth century, a chronicle (not extant) was drawn up in Wessex from numerous sources, some of which have been identified † ; other sources are postulated to account for other material ; thus the comparative frequency of West Saxon entries down to 754 and a paucity of such entries for the period 755–823 suggests that the compiler had a set of West Saxon annals down to the year 754 ; the five West Saxon entries between 755 and 823 may in a few cases have been derived from oral, but in other cases written, tradition.‡ After 823, the English material is contemporary with the compilation

* With the exception of F all these versions have been printed at various times ; the most important editions are Thorpe's (which prints A[1], B, C, D, E, and parts of F, sometimes with silent alterations of the MSS), Plummer's (which prints MSS A[1] and E in full, with occasional extracts from the rest) and Classen and Harmer (MS D, very carefully reproduced) ; Plummer's is the standard text, but there are some errors of transcription, such as 836 *fultumode* (MS *fultomode*), 837[1] *aldorman* (MS *aldormon*), 840 *wælstowe* (MS *pelstope*), 887[18] *drefde* (MS *dræfde*), 890 *butueoh* (MS *betueoh*), 894[7] *sio* (MS *seo*), 894[14], 895[1] *ylcan* (MS *ilcan*), 895[6] *pare* (MS *þære*), 895[9] *be þære eæ* (MS *bi þære éæ*), 895[14] *scypu* (MS *scipu*), 896[25] *mycel* (MS *micel*), 896[39] *eodan* (MS *eodon*), 896[52] *þam* (MS *þæm*), &c.

† Such as Bede's *Historia Ecclesiastica* and its chronological summary (Bk V, cap. xxiv), a continuation of this down to Ecgberht, genealogical lists of Northumbrian and Mercian kings, &c ; cf Plummer II. cix.

‡ Cf H. M. Chadwick, *Origin of the English Nation* (Cambridge 1924) 26, and F. P. Magoun, Anglia xlv. 24 ff.

of the original chronicle in the sense that it was incorporated within living memory of the events. The records of foreign events, especially for the years 880–c.890, may have been drawn from contemporary continental annals.

The date when this original chronicle was compiled is uncertain. The first hand of MS A[1] carries us down to the year 891 ; this scribe adds the year-number 892 but made no entry (see notes *infra*, p. 40) ; the annal 891 was completed later by the second scribe. This suggests that 891 was the date when the first part of the Parker MS was written and therefore the latest at which the original chronicle could have been compiled. Certainly up to this point all the extant versions have a common source. But there may have been still earlier recensions. There was possibly one which finished at 887, for Asser only uses a version of the Chronicle down to that year.* There was possibly an older version still, for the genealogy of Æþelwulf given immediately after the death of Æþelwulf in the annal 855 looks like the termination of such a recension,† which was brought up to date in Ælfred's reign and carried on at intervals to 891. It is almost impossible to reconstruct the character of the lost original, whatever its date, for not even the oldest of the extant versions, the Parker MS, gives by itself a clear picture of its prototype,‡ whilst it seems likely that a version of the Chronicle

* Cf M. L. R. Beaven, EHR xxxiii. 331, n. 13. If this is true, then material must have been added to the annal 887, which in its extant form could not have been written before Spring 889 (cf notes to 887 *infra*, p. 38).

† Cf F. M. Stenton, *Essays presented to T. F. Tout* (Manchester 1925), 15, note 2. Professor Stenton says, on the other hand, that it is hard to believe that the ' hallowing ' of Ælfred as king (in 853) could have been recorded before Ælfred's accession in 871. But this is only a difficulty if we accept the chronicler's statement at its face value ; see, however, 853[8] (note).

‡ The Parker MS has several errors, such as *Cariei* for *Caziei* (887) and some omissions (in 853, 874), and in 851 it arranges its material in a different order from the other MSS. That A[1] is a copy (to 891) is proved by the scribal error in 845 (see textual note to 845).

used by Ethelwerd contained more material than any of the extant manuscripts.*

The version of the Chronicle drawn up in Ælfred's reign has long been associated by scholars with Ælfred and Winchester. This version, as we have seen, belongs to 887, or at the latest to 891, and as Ælfred is known to have inspired literary activity about that time he may well have ordered an older recension of the chronicle to be brought up to date. But the only evidence we have is in the twelfth-century Gaimar's *L'Estorie des Engles* (ed. T. D. Hardy, Rolls Series, I., ll. 3451–2), *Il fist escrivere un livre Engleis Des aventures e des leis*. From the association of the annals with the laws, Plummer (II. cv, note) rightly concluded that Gaimar knew a manuscript of the Chronicle like A[1] where the Chronicle and the Laws are found together. That the attribution to Ælfred should be found only in the version of the Chronicle to which Gaimar had access is unlikely and it is probably no more than a guess by Gaimar based upon his knowledge that the Laws were called the Laws of Ælfred. A further connexion with Ælfred has also been suggested on the grounds of close verbal parallels between the Chronicle and the Old English Orosius,† but these parallels are such as would be expected in works with similar themes, and in any case many of them are found in the post-Ælfredian section. At the most these similarities of expression could only prove that the Chronicler and the translator of the Orosius were familiar with each other's work. Furthermore, Ælfred may not have stood alone in his patronage of learning and literature ; ' personal reasons, not now to be discovered, may have led some particular noble of the ninth century to wish for a vernacular rendering of earlier English history '.‡ The objections raised are against the type of evidence used to prove that Ælfred

* Cf F. M. Stenton, *op. cit.* 20–1.

† Plummer II. cvi–cvii. Those in the annals 832–900 are cited in the notes to 865, 867, 871, 879, 891, 893.

‡ F. M. Stenton, *op. cit.* 23.

himself wrote the Chronicle ; such objections, however, cannot prove and, indeed, are not intended to prove that Ælfred could not have been the compiler. He may have participated in the compilation of the Chronicle, but we cannot prove it. At the same time, it seems likely that he should have sponsored it in some way or other. The textual history of the different versions suggests that the ' Ælfredian ' Chronicle was circulated throughout the kingdom, and on the analogy of the *Cura Pastoralis* (cf below, p. 9 note) it is likely, as an ' official ' document, to have had the king's sanction.

The association of the original chronicle with Winchester is equally uncertain. The chief evidence is again provided by Gaimar,* whose statement was without doubt based upon the view (also held by some modern writers) that Winchester was Ælfred's capital. It is commonly held † that Winchester was the ' national ' capital as well as the ecclesiastical centre of Wessex and therefore the likely home of a ' national ' chronicle. But in a very lucid discussion of this problem Professor Stenton (*op. cit.* 15 ff) has shewn that the importance of Winchester belongs to the tenth and eleventh centuries, not the ninth, and that in the ninth century it is improbable that Wessex had any definite capital. Moreover, the chronicle as we know it is far from being a ' national ' chronicle—a character ascribed to it, perhaps, to explain the infrequency of Winchester entries (855 and 860 are amongst the few). On the contrary, the local interest is at times strongly developed, but then it is always centred on Dorset and

---

* *Croniz ad nun, un livere grant : Engleis l'alerent asemblant. Ore est issi auctorizez, Ka Wincestre, en l'eveskez, La est des reis la dreite estorie E les vies e la memorie* (Gaimar, *ed. cit.* ll. 2331–6). Cf also Plummer II. cxii. Earle (in his edition of the Chronicle, p. xi) supposed that the association with Winchester is strengthened by the regular record of the Bishops of Winchester 634–754. This, however, is probably derived from an independent series of West Saxon annals (cf above, p. 5, and H. M. Chadwick, *op. cit.* 26). It is significant that the series is broken at 754.

† Plummer II. cxii ; A. Brandl, *Pauls Grundriss* III. 1057, 1071.

Somerset ; it is observed mainly in the preservation of names of obscure places and persons from this south-western region (cf 845, 851, and especially 878), but perhaps more significant is the annal 867 recording the death of Ealhstan, bishop of Sherborne ; the annal adds that ' his body lies there *on tune* ', a detail which only an annalist knowing Sherborne well would find of enough interest to insert in his chronicle.* On such grounds it is not unreasonable to suppose that the Ælfredian recension of the Chronicle was made in the south-west and that copies were circulated from there to different parts of the country † ; that is why there is so much resemblance between some of the extant versions down to about 891. Sometimes, these copies were revised with the incorporation of local material. From time to time new contemporary matter was officially circulated, occasionally supplemented by local information. Fresh copies were made and sent to other places where new local material was added, and no doubt these localized versions were used to bring up to date copies in other places. The manuscripts that have survived are for the most part transcripts of such copies and from these circumstances their textual relationship is complex. There is, however, contemporary or nearly contemporary material of the ninth and tenth centuries in MS A[1], and of the eleventh and twelfth centuries in MS E.

Chronology

It might be expected that a chronicle which takes an order of years for its framework would be accurate in its chronological information, but such is not the case with the

---

* Cf also 878[17] note.

† The circulation of manuscripts of the Chronicle would be analogous to the distribution of copies of the *Cura Pastoralis* intended by Ælfred : *to ælcum biscepstole on minum rice wille* [*ic*] *ane onsendan* (ed. H. Sweet, EETS xlv, 6). It is quite possible that the Parker MS itself down to 891 was such a copy made in the south-west ; it becomes a chronicle with a Winchester interest only after 891 (see above, p. 3).

Old English Chronicle. In the series of annals 754–845 the events are recorded two years and in some annals (829–39, possibly to 845) three years too early. This error was not in the original version, for an archaic manuscript of the chronicle used in the Annals of St Neots was apparently free from it *; but since it appears in all extant manuscripts of the chronicle it was no doubt made in an early recension, where the scribe wrongly omitted to pass over two annals 754 and 756 for which there should have been no entries. The error is corrected at 851, as a series of blank annals 846–50 made a return to the true chronology possible.

A second error whereby events are recorded one year too late occurs in the annals 892–928 in MS A[1] only. The original scribes copied the annals under the proper years, but in the tenth century mistaken ' corrections ' were made by scribes who added 1 to each of the dominical years in this series.†

A third set of inconsistencies in dating events is more complex, but an explanation has been put forward in a very scholarly fashion by the late M. L. R. Beaven,‡ to shew why only certain events in an annal appear to be recorded a year too late. Actually the annalistic year under which an event was recorded depended upon the date at which the annalist's year began. In mediaeval times the year could begin (in relation to our present practice of starting it on 1 January) on (1) the Annunciation (25 March) preceding 1 January (the so-called *Stylus Pisanus*), (2) 1 September preceding 1 January (the Constantinople Indiction), (3) 24 September preceding

* Cf L. Theopold, *Kritische Untersuchungen* (1872), 53, 85, Plummer II. cii, ciii, and Stevenson 105–6.

† See notes to 891 [14], 892, below. In this edition the dates given by the original scribes have been restored, 892 being treated as part of the annal 891, 893 as 892, and so on. Similarly all references are to these restored dates. This has so far been done by only one scholar, Professor R. W. Chambers, in his *England before the Norman Conquest* (1926).

‡ EHR xxxiii. 328–42.

1 January (the Caesarean Indiction), (4) 25 December (Christmas Day, Mid-Winter's Day) before 1 January, (5) 1 January, and (6) the Annunciation after 1 January (the *Stylus Florentinus*).* Of these possible beginnings Bede and the older parts of the Chronicle use the Caesarean Indiction of 24 September, and from about 890 the Chronicle also uses the Christmas beginning (see notes *ad loc.*), but not exclusively (cf 900 note). These facts are not self-evident, for only by correlation with data from other sources can the obscure chronology of the Chronicle be explained. The relevant difficulties are these : from 878 foreign events are often recorded one year too late ; thus the autumnal movement of the Danes to Ghent recorded under 880 belongs to November 879, the movement to the Meuse recorded in 882 to November 881, and so on (see notes to 880, 881, 882, 883, 884, 885 and 885[15], 886[2], 887, 890[6]). Earle and Plummer, who assumed a Christmas beginning for most parts of the Chronicle, suggested that this series of annals 879–87 (see 879 n) was one year out, but this took no account of foreign events which are correctly dated in those annals, as, for example, the Battle with the Franks of August 881, correctly recorded under 881. If, however, the year began at the September Indiction events which took place between 24 September and 31 December would naturally be entered under what is to us the following year. The evidence for such a beginning is clear. In many of the annals the first recorded event is the autumnal movement of the Danes into winter-quarters. Again, in the annal 885 the death of Louis is said to have occurred in the year of the sun's eclipse, the eclipse being already recorded under 879. This eclipse was on 29 October, 878, and Louis' death on 10 April,

* See further R. L. Poole, *The Beginning of the Year in Mediæval Times* (Proceedings of the British Academy, X (1921), (reprinted in R. L. Poole, *Studies in Chronology and History*, (Oxford) 1934) ; R. L. Poole, *Medieval Reckonings of Time*, 1918. Plummer also assumes an Easter beginning, but the instances given by him are merely examples of the Stylus Florentinus (cf Beaven 329).

879 (see notes to 879, 885[15]) ; these two dates were clearly within one annalistic year, which must therefore have commenced between 11 April and 28 October. Similarly the chronological details in the annal 871 shew that the year began between the end of May and 28 December and those in 878 that it began between 6 July and 7 January (see notes to 878[1], 878[10]) ; the final events in the annal 877 carry the earlier limiting date to 7 August (see note to 877[10]). Putting this evidence together, we can determine that the year began somewhere between 7 August and 28 October ; we may guess that the year actually began at the Caesarean Indiction of 24 September, for there is no evidence that the Constantinople Indiction of 1 September was ever used in England.

This establishment of the beginning of the annalist's year does not materially alter the chronological development of Ælfred's campaigns, but it does explain inconsistencies in the recording of foreign events and some obscurities in the movements of the Danes. It enables us, for example, to put the first wintering of the Danes in Thanet recorded in 851 in the late autumn of 850 and therefore before their defeat at *Aclea* in 851 ; this defeat was so overwhelming that nothing more is heard of the Danes until 853, and meanwhile Burȝred of Mercia and king Æþelwulf subdued the Welsh. It is unlikely that this Welsh campaign would have been attempted had the defeated Danes gone into winter-quarters in the autumn of 851. Other annals which also become clearer in the light of an annalistic year beginning on 24 September are 868, 870, 872, 874, 878, 879, 900.

LANGUAGE OF THE PARKER MS

The orthography and phonology of the Parker MS throws little light on its place of origin, but judging by the preservation of occasional archaisms in proper names drawn from versions of the Chronicle used by Asser and in the Annals of St Neots,* the Parker MS down to 891 was a somewhat modernized version ; it is thus one of the principal sources for the study of West Saxon of the second half of the ninth century.

The most significant feature is the change of orthography that accompanied a change in handwriting. In the first hand down to 891, *ð* is almost unknown (*broður* 871, *ðeron* 882, *ðæm* 891), *þ* being the usual symbol ; *ð* is found more frequently after 891 and becomes common in 894. The letter *ę* is usual down to 891, though *æ* is found occasionally and *Ae* once (*Aelfred* 885) ; *æ* only is used after 891. Other archaic spellings in the first hand include an occasional *u*, *uu* for *p* (*cuom*, *tueʒen*, *uuoldon* 878), and the frequent use of *u* for later *o* in unstressed syllables (*ʒefenʒun* 851, *broþur* 860, *ʒebocude* 855). Older phonological forms in the first hand include the retention of *u* in *cuom* (*com* in later hands, as 893), final *ʒ* remaining voiced in *ofsloʒ* 885 (later *ofsloh*), and the retention of the diphthong *io* (later *eo*), as in *elþiodiʒnesse* 891, *sio* 885 ; the second hand, it may be noted, has one or two *io* forms, as *sio* besides *seo* in 893. The characteristic West Saxon diphthong *ie* is found almost invariably down to 891, as *unieþelice* 878, *apiestrode* 879, *fierd*, but after 891 later WSax or non-WSax variants are found, as *uneðelice* 896, *fird* 895. Before 891 *a* before *l* + consonant generally remains unbroken, as *ʒepald* 833, *salde* 836, *aldormon* 837, *alle* 853, *haldanne* 874, apart from a rare broken form like *healdan* 887, but after 891 broken forms are regular, as *ealle* 892, *sealde* 893, *ealdormon* 893, &c. The unbroken forms of the first hand may be Anglian in origin, due possibly to some Anglian scholar, who like Pleʒemund (see note to 890[9]) had sought patronage in Wessex, or they may be a relic of a more archaic WSax spelling tradition ;

---

* Cf *Coenred* (*oe* from *i*-mutation of *ō*, later *ē*) ; **Guuihtgara-burhg** (containing the old gen.sg. *-gāra* from *-gār*, an old *u*-stem, later *-gares* ; cf Parker MS *þihtʒarasburʒ*) ; **Koenuualh** (later *Cēn*-), *Oisc* (later replaced by *Æsc*). See Stevenson lxxxv, 105, 173.

but non-WSax forms are otherwise very rare * before 891 ; on the other hand, archaic spellings already noted, as well as *efor* 885 (which would be archaic in any dialect), support the second alternative.†

With the later hands the orthography is more varied and though in the second hand there are a few stray archaisms like *porhtun* (later *-on*), *ȝepaldenum* (later *-ea-*), *ȝeporct* ‡ (later *-ht*) 893, there are many spellings usually associated with WSax of the tenth century, as *sæde* (for *sæȝde*) 893, *þena* (for *þeȝna* 896), *betpuh* 893 (cf *betueoh* 889), *pucena* 893 (cf older *piecan* 878), *cinȝes* 893 (older *cyninȝes*), and occasional forms (besides those in *ie* already mentioned) with diphthongs simplified (perhaps on Anglian models), as *ȝeperc* 895, *þeh* (*conj.*) 893, 896, *mehte* 893, &c, *mehton* 893, &c, *ȝere* 894, &c (cf *ȝepeorc* 868, *þeah* (*adv.*) 867, *meahte* 877, *ȝeare*).

In its style the Chronicle is generally clear and simple. Through the recurrence of events of a similar kind there is a tendency towards the constant use of stereotyped phrases such as *ahton pælstope ȝepald, siȝe namon*, &c, but in spite of this the diction is varied. Further, the traditional notion of a chronicle would offer little scope for the skilful and artistic unfolding of a story, but the exposition is not monotonous, and for one of the earliest specimens of free

* The only noteworthy one is *piotan* 853, 868 (with Kentish or Anglian back-mutation, WSax *pitan*).

† Unfortunately the evidence for very early WSax is scanty, but, in the few charters, we have broken and unbroken forms in proper names, as OET 427 no. 2 (693–731) *ualdharius* ; 427 no. 3 (778) *-healh, egcbaldus* ; 434 no. 20 (847) *denewaldes stan, fordeqlf, healdanweg, wealdenesford, se alda suinhaga, alhstan.* The earliest West Saxon orthography may have been modelled to a considerable extent on Anglian. There is in later times no evidence to support Luick's conjecture (*Historische Grammatik*, § 146 n. 2) that in some WSax dialects there was sound-development similar to that in Anglian.

‡ It is doubtful whether this is really archaic ; a simple spelling mistake is more likely, for the scribe wrote *ȝepeorc* at the end of fol. 17a and then wrote *ȝeporc* (for *ȝeporht*) at the beginning of fol. 17b ; it was corrected by adding *t*. See textual note 893[59].

prose composition in the language and one largely independent of Latin influence the variety of expression and
the restraint shewn by the chronicler are remarkable.

The sentences, especially the compound sentences, are of a
primitive type ; parataxis is the rule and hypotaxis the exception.[*]
But although the style is simple and occasionally ambiguous, there
is a fair range in sentence-structures. The most characteristic
types include : (1) The simple sentence often introduced by an
adverb or adverbial expression with the finite verb before the
subject, as *Her for se here up on Sunnan* 884 or *þy ilcan ʒeare æt
middum pintra forþferde Carl Francna cyninʒ* 885, though where
the subject is plural the normal order of subject and predicate is
often kept, as *On þa ea hi tuʒon up hiora scipu* 892. (2) A succession
of such sentences joined by *ond*, as 7 *þy ilcan ʒeare ʒebocude Æþelpulf cyninʒ teo þan dǫl his londes . . . 7 þy ilcan ʒeare ferde to Rome . . . .
7 þær pas xii monaþ puniende . . .* 855. (3) A rarer type of simple
sentence introduced by subject and predicate, as *Seo ea . . . lið ut
of þæm pealda* 892. (4) A simple sentence with the order of subject and finite verb reversed (rare), as *Næfde se here, ʒodes þonces,
Angelcyn ealles forspiþe ʒebrocod* 896, *Þæs Hæsten þa þær cumen.
Hæfde Hæsten ær ʒeporht þæt ʒepeorc* 893. (5) The common
type of compound or correlative sentence where the subordinate
clause is introduced by a conjunction with the subject and verb
in the order subject + verb and the principal sentence with or
without correlative adverb and subject and verb in reversed
order (as *Þa hie þa hampeard pendon, þa metton hie micelne
sciphere* 855. *Þa he þa pæs hiderpeardes 7 sio oþeru fierd hampeardes . . . , þa ʒeʒaderedon þa þe in Norþhymbrum buʒeað . . . .
sum hund scipa* 893).

---

[*] See G. Rübens, *Parataxe und Hypotaxe* (1915) ; the best study
of the style of the Chronicle is G. C. Donald, *Zur Entwicklung des
Prosastils in der Sachsenchronik* (1914).

The punctuation is modern. The use of capitals is modern (with a few exceptions capitals in the MS are confined to the first word of an annal) ; in proper names the MS normally uses small initials ; in this text *Æ* (initially in proper names) represents MS *ę* down to 891 (fol. 16a), thereafter *æ*. Abbreviations are expanded : ∼ as *m* (*nam*, MS *nã* 853[8] ; *hampeard*, MS *hãpeard* 855[6] ; &c) and as *n* rarely (*porhtun*, MS *porhtũ* 893[68]) ; ' as *e* (ɉ' = ɉe, *tpeɉ'n* = *tpeɉen* ; *moniɉ'* = *moniɉe* 838[4] ; *fierd'* = *fierde* 851[10] ; *hæfd'* = *hæfde* 885[28] ; *h'* = *he* 878[29]) ; ' as *ep* (*bisc'(rice)* = *biscep(rice)* 845[2], 867[13] &c) ; ' as *er* (*pint'* = *pinter* 855[2] ; *æft'* = *æfter* 878[21] ; &c) and as *re* (*pint'* = *pintre* 870[2]) ; Latin words when abbreviated are expanded as in C. Trice Martin, *Record Interpreter* (London 1910). Additions above or below the line (as *ɉefeaht*, *t* above, 845 ; *fenɉon*, *on* above, 855[30] ; *adrencton*, *n* above *ct*, 890[9] ; *miercna*, *a* below, 851[9] ; *his*, *i* below, 851[10] ; &c) made by the original scribe of the particular annal are not noted except where the correction has interest. The year numbers (always Roman numerals) are usually in the left-hand margin as disposed in the printed text. In the text of the MS there is down to 891 no indentation by the year numbers ; as far as is consistent with economy of space, variations in the size of margin are indicated by spaces at the beginnings of the lines in this text. Some tribal names (*Suþ-Seaxe*, *Norþ-Ɖalas*, &c) are hyphened in this text ; the two elements are generally separate words in the MS.

THE PARKER CHRONICLE

(Corpus Christi College, Cambridge, MS 173, fol. 12a–20a)

Anno dcccxxxii. Her heþne men oferherȝeadon Sceapiȝe.

Anno dcccxxxiii. Her ȝefeaht Ecȝbryht cyninȝ þiþ xxxu
   sciphlæsta æt Carrum 7 þær pearþ micel þel ȝeslæȝen,
   7 þa Denescan ahton þelstope ȝepald ; 7 Hereferþ
   7 Þiȝþen tueȝen biscepas forþferdon, 7 Dudda 7
   Osmod tueȝen aldormen forþferdon.

Anno dcccxxxu. Her cuom micel sciphere on Þest-Þalas
   7 hie to anum ȝecierdon, 7 þiþ Ecȝbryht Þest
   Seaxna cyninȝ pinnende pæron. Þa he þæt hierde
   7 mid fierde ferde 7 him þiþ feaht æt Henȝestdune
   7 þær ȝefliemde ȝe þa Þalas ȝe þa Deniscan.

TEXTUAL VARIANTS : 833. Below 833 in margin is *A ñ dcccxxxiiii*

---

832. Actually 835 (cf Introd. p. 9). Apart from the isolated
reference in 787, this is the first mention of the Danes in this version of the Chronicle. In 834 the Danes had been harrying in the
Netherlands (cf *Annales Xantenses*, ed. B. de Simson, Hannover
1909, p. 9), and the raid on Sheppey may have been made by the
same fleet. There was in later years a close connexion between
the English and Continental operations of the Danes (cf, for instance,
880, 885, 892).

833. Actually 836. 35 ship-crews would be about 700 to 1000
men ; *æt Carrum* is Carhampton, Somerset (cf B. Dickins, *Times
Literary Suppl.* 22 Sept. 1922, Mawer 46).

835. Actually 838. [2] *hie to anum ȝecierdon : hie* = the Cornish
and the Danes. On this and other alliances of the Cornish men
and the Danes cf B. G. Charles, *Old Norse Relations with Wales*
(Cardiff 1934), 2, and A. F. Major, *Early Wars of Wessex* (Cambridge 1913), 83. Cornwall hoped to throw off the Saxon domination, whilst it was not itself an attractive objective to the Danes
except for the men the latter could obtain for their raids on Wessex.

[3] *pinnende pæron :* note the progressive form ' continued fighting '; it is not frequent in OE ; cf also 867[7], 876.

Anno dcccxxxui. Her Ecʒbryht cyninʒ forþferde, 7 hine
  hæfde ær Offa Miercna cyninʒ 7 Beorhtric Þesseaxna
  cyninʒ afliemed xiii ʒear of Anʒelcynnes lande on
  Fronclond, ær he cyninʒ pære, 7 þy fultomode
  Beorhtric Offan þy he hæfde his dohtor him to ⁵
  cuene ; 7 se Ecʒbryht ricsode xxxuii pintra, uii
  monaþ, 7 fenʒ Æþelpulf Ecʒbrehtinʒ to Þesseaxna
  rice, 7 he salde his suna Æþelstane Cantpara rice
  7 East-Seaxna 7 Suþriʒea 7 Suþ-Seaxna.
Anno dcccxxxuii. Her Þulfheard aldormon ʒefeaht æt
  Hamtune piþ xxxiii sciphlæsta 7 þær micel pæl
  ʒesloʒ 7 siʒe nom. 7 þy ʒeare forþferde Þulfheard.
  7 þy ilcan ʒeare ʒefeaht Æþelhelm dux piþ Deniscne
  here on Port mid Dornsætum 7 ʒode hpile þone ⁵
  here ʒefliemde, 7 þa Deniscan ahton pælstope
  ʒepald 7 þone aldormon ofsloʒon.

836³. *xiii*, MS *iii*. 836⁴. *pære* begins fol. 12b.

---

836. Actually 839. ³ *hæfde :* note the singular form followed by
double subject, as in 875⁵. ² *ær....ær he cyninʒ pære,* ' on a pre-
vious occasion thirteen years before he was to be king '. On the
correction of MS *iii* to *xiii* cf Plummer II. 75.

⁸ *his suna Æþelstane,* Ecʒbryht's son Æþelstan.

837. Probably 840. ¹ *aldormon ;* the function of this high official
was to act as the king's principal deputy in a large district (cf H. M.
Chadwick, *Studies on Anglo-Saxon Institutions* (1905), 163, 282, 289).

⁵ *here,* hereafter the usual name for the Danish army ; in the
Laws of Ine a band of robbers numbering 7 to 35 was called a *hloþ*
(cf 893¹¹), and a band numbering 35 or more was called a *here*
(F. L. Attenborough, *Laws of the Earliest English Kings,* Cambridge
1922, p. 40).

⁸ *7 ʒode hpile þone here ʒefliemde :* there is an apparent contra-
diction in the Danes being put to flight and yet gaining possession
of the battlefield ; so also in 871²⁵ ; cf Hoffmann-Hirtz 66n, G.
Rübens, *Parataxe und Hypotaxe* (1915), 20. MSS D and E substi-
tute for this another phrase (7 *se ealdorman pærð ofslæʒen*), which
makes the Danish victory clearer. In this version, however, the
passage probably means that ' for a long time they drove back
the Danes, but ultimately the Danes won the battle '. In the 871
example the same explanation may hold, but in any case the language is there ambiguous.

Anno dcccxxxuiii.   Her Herebryht aldormon pæs ofslæʒen
from heþnum monnum 7 moniʒe mid him on
Merscparum, 7 þy ilcan ʒeare eft on Lindesse 7 on
East-Enʒlum 7 on Cantparum purdon moniʒe men
ofslæʒene from þam heriʒe.

Anno dcccxxxuiiii.   Her pæs micel pelsliht on Lundenne 7
on Cpantapic 7 on Hrofesceastre.

Anno dcccxl.   Her Æþelpulf cyninʒ ʒefeaht æt Carrum piþ
xxxu sciphlæsta, 7 þa Deniscan a hton pelstope ʒepald.

Anno dcccxlu.   Her Eanulf aldorman ʒefeaht mid Sumur-
sætum 7 Ealchstan biscep 7 Osric aldorman mid
Dornsætum ʒefuhton æt Pedridan muþan piþ Deniscne here 7 þær micel pel ʒesloʒon 7 siʒe namon.

840. The annal years in the margin are in an unbroken series to
852 ; the annal 840 takes 2 lines and is therefore opposite 840 and
841 ; 842, 843, 844 are blank ; the annal 845 in 3 lines is opposite
the year numbers 845, 846, 847 ; 848, 849, 850 are blank ; the first
two lines of the annal 851 are opposite the year numbers 851, 852.

845. A sentence has been erased at the end of this annal, but
enough remains to shew that the scribe has wrongly added here
the second sentence of 851, where it follows a sentence similar to
that in 845 ; the words now visible are | 7 *þy ilcanʒ......þelstan......
ealhchere dux......ofsloʒon | æt Sondpic on kent 7 uiiii scipu ʒefenʒun
7 þa oþre ʒefliemdon |.*

---

838. Actually 841. *Herebryht* was an aldorman of Mercia and
Merscparum may refer to the ' people of the marshlands ' of Lincoln-
shire, rather than to Romney Marsh (Kent), suggested by Plummer
II. 412 ; *eft* in l. 3 may have the force of ' again in Lindsey '.   But
Mersc (MS A), *Merscpare* (MS E &c) certainly refer to Romney
Marsh in 796.

839. Actually 842. *Cpantapic*, probably Quentowic, a lost place
near Étaples, destroyed by the Danes in 842 (Hoffmann-Hirtz
67n, Plummer II. 76).

840. Probably 843, or possibly 844 (according to L. Theopold,
Kritische Untersuchungen (1872), 61). From 843 to 848 the Danes
were engaged in raids on the Continent ; this probably explains
the absence of entries in the Chronicle between 840 and 845.
There is a great similarity between this annal and 833, but since
it is found in this form in all Chronicles there is no reason to doubt
its authenticity (cf Plummer II. 76).

845. Probably 848. *æt Pedridan muþan*, mouth of the R. Parrett, Somerset.

Anno dcccli. Her Ceorl aldormon ʒefeaht piþ hæþene
men mid Defenascire æt Þicʒanbeorʒe, 7 þær micel
pɇl ʒesloʒon 7 siʒe namon. 7 þy ilcan ʒeare Æþelstan cyninʒ 7 Ealchere dux micelne here ofsloʒon
æt Sondpic on Cent 7 ix scipu ʒefenʒun 7 þa oþre   5
ʒefliemdon. 7 hɇþne men ærest ofer pinter sæton.
7 þy ilcan ʒeare cuom feorðe healf hund scipa on
Temese muþan 7 brɇcon Contparaburʒ 7 Lundenburʒ, 7 ʒefliemdon Beorhtpulf Miercna cyninʒ mid
his fierde, 7 foron þa suþ ofer Temese on Suþriʒe   10
7 him ʒefeaht piþ Æþelpulf cyninʒ 7 Æþelbald his
sunu æt Aclea mid Þest-Seaxna fierde, 7 þær þæt
mæste pɇl ʒesloʒon on hɇþnum heriʒe þe pe secʒan
hierdon oþ þisne ondþeardan dæʒ, 7 þær siʒe namon.

851⁷. *feorðe : rðe* added above the line by another hand ; *eo*
also appears to be a correction.   851¹⁴. MS 7 *peardan.*

851ₐ The true chronology is restored (see Introd. pₐ 10). The
raid on Devonshire may have been a move to distract the West
Saxons from the great invasion on the east (l. 6). But the fights
at *Þicʒanbeorʒe* and Sandwich probably took place in the autumn
of 850. The Danes then went into winter-quarters and in the
spring of 851 the great invasion took place. The Danes were then
defeated at *Aclea* and probably left the country (cf Introd. p. 12).

² *æt Þicʒanbeorʒe ;* the identity is uncertain ; Weekaborough
(Devon) and Wigborough (Somerset) have been proposed and
there is nothing in the early spellings of these names to rule out
either (cf Stevenson 176, *Place-Names of Devon* (EPN IX), 506),
though those of Wigborough agree more closely with *Þicʒanbeorʒe.*
Wigborough is not in Devonshire, but it is only 5 miles outside and
Stevenson (l.c.) notes that ' the *fyrd* is occasionally found fighting
outside its county '.

⁸ *Lundenburʒ :* London was still under Mercian rule ; it was
recaptured by Ælfred in 886.

¹¹ *him ʒefeaht piþ Æþelpulf . . . :* as usual when the verb precedes a multiple subject it takes the number of the first part of the
subject ; cf 853¹ (see textual note to 853²), where a later scribe has
added *bædon* as an alternative to the original singular form *bɇd.*

¹² *Aclea :* Ockley (Surrey) has been suggested by Plummer II.
78, but the early spellings of this name do not accord with *Aclea*
(*Place-Names of Surrey* (EPN X), 208, 276). The name is common
in OE and as the Chronicle gives no other clue the choice of the
right Oakley must remain uncertain (Mawer 44).

Anno dcccliii. Her bed Burȝred Miercna cyninȝ 7 his
    piotan Æþelpulf cyninȝ þæt he him ȝefultumade
    þæt him Norþ-Palas ȝehiersumade. He þa spa
    dyde, 7 mid fierde fór ofer Mierce on Norþ-Palas,
    7 hie him alle ȝehiersume dydon. 7 þy ilcan ȝeare   5
    sende Æþelpulf cyninȝ Ælfred his sunu to Rome.
    Þa pas domine Leo papa on Rome, 7 he hine to
    cyninȝe ȝehalȝode 7 hiene him to biscepsuna nam.
    Þa þy ilcan ȝeare Ealhere mid Cantparum 7 Huda
    mid Suþriȝium ȝefuhton on Tenet piþ heþnum   10
    heriȝe 7 ærest siȝe namon, 7 þær pearþ moniȝ
    mon ofslæȝen 7 adruncen on ȝehpeþere hond.
    Ond þæs ofer Eastron ȝeaf Æþelpulf cyninȝ his
    dohtor Burȝrede cyninȝe of Pesseaxum on Merce.
Anno dccclu. Her heþne men ærest on Sceapiȝe ofer
    pinter sætun. 7 þy ilcan ȝeare ȝebocude Æþelpulf
    cyninȝ teoþan del his londes ofer al his rice Ȝode

853². *eþelpulf* begins fol. 13a. In the margin is the date *añ
dcccliiii* ; a later hand has added *bædon* above *eþelpulf* ; *he*, MS
he he. 853⁶. A cross in margin opposite Ælfred's name. 853⁷.
domine, papa, MS *dõne, pãp*. 853⁹. *Huda mid*, MS *hudamid*, with
a stroke below *a* to separate the words. 853¹⁴. *Ond*, MS *O'*.

855. On this and the next four lines of the margin of this annal
are the year numbers 855 to 859. 855³. *Ȝode*, MS *ȝo*.

853³. *him* may be singular ' him ' (i.e. Burȝred) or plural ' them '
(i.e. Burȝred and Æþelpulf in alliance).

⁶ *to cyninȝe ȝehalȝode :* Ælfred would now be 5 years old, for the
preface to the Chronicle says that he was 23 years old when he
became king in 871. The actual ceremony was apparently the
investing of Ælfred by Pope Leo IV with the robes and belt of consul
(see Leo's letter, cited by Plummer II. 79) and confirmation in the
faith. Perhaps the assertion that he was ' hallowed as king ' was
a misinformed rumour current in England, and possibly some such
report may have led to Æþelbald's revolt against his father Æþelwulf in 855 (Asser), about which the Chronicle is curiously silent.
Such a misunderstanding explains why Æþelbald could be granted
the rule of the western part of his father's kingdom after his revolt.

¹¹ *ærest siȝe namon :* it is not clear which side won.

¹⁴ *of Pesseaxum . . . ,* ' as from Wessex to Mercia '.

855³. *teoþan del his londes,* ' a tenth part of his private lands ' ;
on this difficult problem cf Stevenson 186 ff. This annal summarizes
the rest of Æþelwulf's reign : his journey to Rome where he

to lofe ⁊ him selfum to ecere hᵉlo, ⁊ þy ilcan ᵹeare
ferde to Rome mid micelre peorþnesse ⁊ þær pas ⁵
xii monaþ puniende ⁊ þa him hampeard fór, ⁊ him
þa Carl Francna cyninᵹ his dohtor ᵹeaf him to
cuene, ⁊ æfter þam to his leodum cuom ⁊ hie þæs
ᵹefæᵹene pærun. ⁊ ymb ii ᵹear þæs ðe he of Francum com he ᵹefór, ⁊ his lic liþ æt Pintanceastre, ¹⁰
⁊ he ricsode niᵹonteoþe healf ᵹear. Ond se Æþelpulf pæs Ecᵹbrehtinᵹ, Ecᵹbryht Ealhmundinᵹ,
Ealhmund Eafinᵹ, Eafa Eoppinᵹ, Eoppa Inᵹildinᵹ ;
Inᵹild pæs Ines broþur Pest-Seaxna cyninᵹes,
þæs þe eft ferde to Sancte Petre ⁊ þær eft his feorh ¹⁵
ᵹesealde ; ⁊ hie pæron Cenredes suna, Cenred pæs
Ceolpaldinᵹ, Ceolpald Cuþainᵹ, Cuþa Cuþpininᵹ,
Cuþpine Ceaulininᵹ, Ceaplin Cynricinᵹ, Cynric
Cerdicinᵹ, Cerdic Elesinᵹ, Elesa Eslinᵹ, Esla Ᵹipisinᵹ,
Ᵹipis Piᵹinᵹ, Piᵹ Freapininᵹ, Freapine Friþoᵹarinᵹ, ²⁰
Friþoᵹar Brondinᵹ, Brond Bᵉldæᵹinᵹ, Bᵉldæᵹ
Podeninᵹ, Poden Friþopaldinᵹ, Friþupald Frea-
pininᵹ, Frealaf Friþupulfinᵹ, Friþupulf Finninᵹ, Fin
Ᵹodpulfinᵹ, Ᵹodpulf Ᵹeatinᵹ, Ᵹeat Tᵉtpainᵹ, Tᵉtpa
Beapinᵹ, Beap Sceldpainᵹ, Sceldpea Heremodinᵹ, ²⁵
Heremod Itermoninᵹ, Itermon Hraþrainᵹ, se pæs
ᵹeboren in þære earce : Noe, Lamach, Matusalem,

855⁹. *of*, MS *on*. 855¹¹. *Ond*, MS *O'*.

855¹⁸. *Cuþpine*, originally *cuþa*, *a* being underdotted and then
erased and *pine* added above the line.

---

remained till 856, his return through France where he contracted
a nominal political marriage with Judith, the twelve-year-old daughter of Carloman, his welcome home (in spite of Æþelbald's revolt),
and his death after two years (in 858).

¹⁰ *Pintanceastre* : according to the *Annals of St Neots* (Stevenson
213), Æþelwulf was first interred at Steyning ; cf F. M. Stenton,
Essays presented to T. F. Tout (1925), 17.

¹¹ On the genealogy of Æþelwulf cf Stevenson 157 ff, R. W.
Chambers, *An Introduction to Beowulf* (2d ed. Cambridge 1932),
195–204, 311–22. Beyond Cerdic, the earliest West Saxon king
mentioned here, we probably have some continental kings, but it is
difficult to say where history merges into myth in this line. *Freapininᵹ* (l. 22) is probably a mistake for *Frealafinᵹ*.

Enoh, Iaered, Maleel, Camon, Enos, Sed, Adam primus homo et pater noster est Christus, Amen. Ond þa fenʒon Æþelpulfes suna tpeʒen to rice, [30] Æþelbald to Þesseaxna rice 7 Æþelbryht to Cantpara rice 7 to East-Seaxna rice 7 to Suþriʒea 7 to Suþ-Seaxna rice ; 7 þa ricsode Æþelbald u ʒear.

Anno dccclx. Her Æþelbald cynʒ forþferde 7 his lic liþ æt Sciraburnan, 7 fenʒ Æþelbryht to allum þam rice his broþur 7 he hit heold on ʒodre ʒeþuærnesse 7 on micelre sibsumnesse. 7 on his dæʒe cuom micel sciphere up 7 abrecon Þintanceastre 7 piþ þone [5] here ʒefuhton Osric aldorman mid Hamtunscire 7 Æþelpulf aldormon mid Bearrucscire, 7 þone here ʒefliemdon 7 pelstope ʒepald ahton. 7 se Æþelbryht ricsode u ʒear 7 his lic liþ æt Scireburnan.

Anno dccclxu. Her sæt heþen here on Tenet 7 ʒenamon friþ piþ Cantparum, 7 Cantpare him feoh ʒeheton piþ þam friþe, 7 under þam friþe 7 þam feohʒehate se here hiene on niht up bestel, 7 oferherʒeade alle Cent eastepearde. [5]

855[30]. *Ond*, MS *O'*.

860. Below 860 in the margin is *añ dccclxi* opposite the second line of the annal 860. 860[4]. *micelre*, MS *micelne*. 860[4]. *micel* begins fol. 13b. 860[5]. The words *up.... pintancst'* are added above the line to replace some deleted on this line (7 *only discernible*) ; some have been deleted above the line after *pintancst'* (7 *piθ......*). In the margin opposite the last three lines of this annal are the year numbers 862, 863, 864.

---

[33] *þa ricsode Æþelbald u ʒear :* he died in 860. His reign would therefore begin in 856, probably on his father's return from Rome ; according to the Annals of St Neots (Stevenson 132) he reigned two and a half years with his father.

860[2]. *Sciraburnan*, Sherborne (Dorset), the seat of one of the West Saxon bishoprics.

[9] *ricsode u ʒear :* as he became king in 860, he probably died towards the end of the summer or in the early autumn of 865, for his brother Æþered's succession is not recorded till 866 (which would start, for the chronicler, in September 865).

865[1]. *ʒenamon friþ . . . up bestel :* Plummer II. cvii compares Orosius (ed. H. Sweet, EETS lxxix, 218) : *he genom friþ wiþ þæt folc 7 hiene siþþan aweg bestæl.* Cf Introd. p. 7.

[2] *feohʒehate :* the first promise of Danegeld for the purchase of peace.

Anno dccclxui. Her fenʒ Æþered Æþelbryhtes broþur to Þesseaxna rice ; 7 þy ilcan ʒeare cuom micel here on Anʒelcynnes lond 7 pintersetl namon on East-Enʒlum 7 þær ʒehorsude purdon 7 hie piþ him friþ namon.   5

Anno dccclxuii. Her fór se here of East-Enʒlum ofer Humbre muþan to Eoforpicceastre on Norþhymbre, 7 þær pæs micel unʒeþuærnes þære þeode betpeox him selfum, 7 hie hæfdun hiera cyninʒ aporpenne Osbryht 7 unʒecyndne cyninʒ underfenʒon Ællan ;   5

866⁴. *piþ* not in MS.

866². *cuom micel here :* this Danish army was led by the sons of Ragnar Lothbrok, the famous Viking. From different sources it appears that these were *Hinguar* (MS F 870, &c = ON *Ivarr inn Bein-lausi* ' the boneless '), *Ubba* (ib. = ODan *Ubbo* in Saxo Grammaticus), *Healfdene* (875-7 *infra*, unknown in Scand. story) ; see also 878 notes. On these vikings cf A. Mawer, *Saga-book of the Viking Society*, vi (1909), 68 ff. The army, which must have come in the autumn of 865 (cf 867 note), remained in England and eventually settled in Northumbria (876), Mercia (877) and East Anglia (880).

⁴ *ʒehorsude purdon :* On the Danish adoption of horses for speed and mobility in traversing the country cf J. H. Clapham, EHR xxv. 287 ; cf also 894, 896, &c below.

867³. *micel unʒeþuærnes :* little is known of these dissensions in Northumbria. Ella, the low-born usurper (863–7), had according to *Ragnar Lothbrok's Saga* caused the death of Ragnar by casting him into a snake pit and it was to avenge this that his sons came to Northumbria. The fall of York was a serious blow to the English, for it remained a Scandinavian possession for many generations. The fight at York took place on the Friday before Palm Sunday (21 March) 867 (Symeon of Durham, *Historiæ Recapitulatio*, Surtees Society 51, p. 70) ; as the preceding union of Ella and Osbryht was already *late on ʒeare*, the movement of the Danes to Northumbria must be placed in the autumn of 866 (Beaven 338, cf Introd. p. 11) ; this would involve putting the wintering in East Anglia (recorded in 866) back to the autumn of 865.

⁶ *hie :* probably Osbryht and Ælla. Cf Symeon of Durham, *Historia Regum* (Surtees Society 51), 48 : *discordia illa sedata est ; rex vero Osbryht et Alla, adunatis viribus, congregatoque exercitu, Eboracum adeunt opidum.*

⁷ *pinnende pærun :* the force of the participle is perhaps progressive and conditional, ' they resolved upon this, that they would continue fighting the marauding army '.

7 hie late on ȝeare to þam ȝecirdon, þæt hie piþ
þone here pinnende pærun, 7 hie þeah micle fierd
ȝeȝadrodon 7 þone here sohton æt Eoforpicceastre
7 on þa ceastre brecon 7 hie sume inne purdon ;
7 þær pas unȝemetlic pel ȝeslæȝen Norþanhymbra, 10
sume binnan, sume butan, 7 þa cyninȝas beȝen
ofslæȝene, 7 sio laf piþ þone here friþ nam. 7 þy
ilcan ȝeare ȝefór Ealchstan biscep 7 he hæfde þæt
bisceprice l pintra æt Scireburnan, 7 his lic liþ
þær on tune.   15

Anno dccclxuiii. Her fór se ilca here innan Mierce to
Snotenȝaham 7 þær pintersetl namon. 7 Burȝred
Miercna cyninȝ 7 his piotan bedon Æþered Pest-
Seaxna cyninȝ 7 Ælfred his broþur þæt hie him
ȝefultumadon, þæt hie piþ þone here ȝefuhton ; 5
7 þa ferdon hie mid Pesseaxna fierde innan Mierce
oþ Snotenȝaham 7 þone here þær metton on þam
ȝepeorce, 7 þær nan hefelic ȝefeoht ne pearþ, 7
Mierce friþ namon piþ þone here.

Anno dccclxix. Her for se here eft to Eoforpicceastre
7 þær sæt i ȝear.

Anno dccclxx. Her rad se here ofer Mierce innan East-
Enȝle 7 pintersetl namon æt Þeodforda. 7 þy pintre

868. A cross in the margin opposite Ælfred's name.
870. 7 *æþered . . . cantuareberi* added by a later scribe.

---

[10] 7 *þær pas unȝemetlic . . . :* Plummer II. cvii compares Orosius :
þær wæs ungemetlic wæl geslagen. Cf Introd. p. 7.

[15] *on tune,* probably ' in the church-yard ' ; the original meaning
of *tun* was ' enclosure ' (A. Mawer, *Chief Elements in English Place-
Names,* EPN I. ii, 61), as in *lic-tun* ' burial ground ', *cyric-tun*
' church yard '. On the sense ' enclosure ' cf OE *ontynan.*

868. The movement of the Danes into winter-quarters at Nottingham was probably in the late autumn of 867 ; it would hardly have
been possible for all the events in this annal to have happened
between the autumn of 868 and the end of 868, even assuming that
the annalist's year began at Christmas ; cf Beaven 336.

870. The Danes moved to Thetford (Norfolk) in the autumn of
869, and Eadmund, therefore, was slain ' in that winter ' of 869–70 ;
Eadmund's death (20 November, according to Abbo of Fleury's
Passio Sancti Eadmundi) could hardly have been in November 870,

Eadmund cyninʒ him piþ feaht 7 þa Deniscan siʒe namon 7 þone cyninʒ ofsloʒon 7 þæt lond all ʒeeodon. 7 þy ʒeare ʒefór Ceolnoþ ærcebiscep ; 7 Æþered Þiltunscire biscop pearþ ʒecoren to ærcebiscpe to Cantuareberi.

Anno dccclxxi. Her cuom se here to Readinʒum on Þest-Seaxe, 7 þæs ymb iii niht ridon ii eorlas up. Þa ʒemette hie Æþelpulf aldorman on Enʒlafelda, 7 him þær piþ ʒefeaht 7 siʒe nam. Þæs ymb iiii niht Æþered cyninʒ 7 Ælfred his broþur þær micle fierd to Readinʒum ʒeleddon 7 piþ þone here

871[7]. -fuhton begins fol. 14a.

---

for that would imply that East Anglia had been subdued and the Danes had moved into Wessex between 20 November 870 and the end of December 870 (cf 871 note and Beaven 336-7).

[3] *Eadmund cyninʒ :* St Edmund, whose martyrdom is related in Abbo of Fleury's *Passio Sancti Eadmundi*, followed by Ælfric in his life of the saint ; cf G. Loomis, *The Growth of the St Edmund Legend*, Harvard Studies in Philology and Literature, xiv (1932), 83-113, and *St Edmund and the Lodbrok legend* (ib. xv, 1933). Eadmund declined to become the vassal king of the pagan, Inguar ; he was therefore bound to a tree, scourged and shot dead with arrows.

[5] *Ceolnoþ*, archbishop of Canterbury, died 4 February 870 (MS D adds *to Rome*).

871. Bishop Heahmund (see l. 28) died 22 March (the date of his obit in the English Calendar) ; from this date the dates of certain battles can be approximately determined (cf Beaven 334-5) : Reading 28 December 870, Englefield 31 December 870, Reading 4 January 871, Ashdown 8 January, Basing 22 January, and, of course, *Meretune* 22 March 871, when Heahmund was slain. The remaining events would be Easter 15 April 871, Æþered's death ' after Easter ' (possibly the second fortnight of April 871), Ælfred at Wilton by the end of May 871. As the first event in this annal is dated 28 December 870, it is usually supposed (Plummer, *Life and Times of Alfred*, 93, Hoffmann-Hirtz 74n) that the annalist changed his year at Christmas 870, but since the Chronicle records no events between 4 February 870 (see 870[5]n) and 28 December 870, there is nothing to shew that he was not following his usual practice of changing his year in September.

[2] *eorlas*, the OE adaptation of ON *jarl*, equivalent as a designation of rank to OE *aldormon* (cf H. M. Chadwick, *Anglo-Saxon Institutions*, 1905, p. 382).

ʒefuhton, 7 þær pæs micel pɛl ʒeslæʒen on ʒe-
hpɛþre hond, 7 Æþelpulf aldormon pearþ ofslæʒen,
7 þa Deniscan ahton pɛlstope ʒepald. 7 þæs
ymb iiii niht ʒefeaht Æþered cyninʒ 7 Ælfred his [10]
broþur piþ alne þone here on Æscesdune, 7 hie
pærun on tpæm ʒefylcum ; on oþrum pæs Bachsecʒ 7 Halfdene þa hɛþnan cyninʒas, 7 on oþrum
pæron þa eorlas. 7 þa ʒefeaht se cyninʒ Æþered
piþ þara cyninʒa ʒetruman 7 þær pearþ se cyninʒ [15]
Baʒsecʒ ofslæʒen, 7 Ælfred his broþur piþ þara eorla
ʒetruman 7 þær pearþ Sidroc eorl ofslæʒen se alda,
7 Sidroc eorl se ʒioncʒa, 7 Osbearn eorl 7 Fræna eorl
7 Hareld eorl ; 7 þa herʒas beʒen ʒefliemde 7 fela
þusenda ofslæʒenra 7 on feohtende pæron oþ niht. [20]
7 þæs ymb xiiii niht ʒefeaht Æþered cyninʒ 7 Ælfred
his broður piþ þone here æt Basenʒum 7 þær þa
Deniscan siʒe namon. 7 þæs ymb ii monaþ ʒefeaht
Æþered cyninʒ 7 Ælfred his broþur piþ þone here
æt Meretune, 7 hie pærun on tuæm ʒefylcium 7 hie [25]

871[11]. A cross in margin, and a small one over *on*.

[11] *on Æscesdune :* the name survives in Ashdown Park in Ash-
bury (Berkshire), but it referred in OE times to a great tract of the
Berkshire Downs (Mawer 44).

[12] *Bachsecʒ :* the names of the Danish leaders here and elsewhere
are discussed by E. Björkman, *Nordische Personennamen in England*
and *Zur englischen Namenkunde* (Halle, 1910, 1912) and J. Jónsson,
Vikingasaga um Herferðir Víkinga (Reykjavik 1915), 103 ; *Bachsecʒ* = ON *Bakskiki* (?), *Halfdene* (cf 862[2]n) = ODan *Halfdanr*,
Sidroc = ON *Sigtryggr* (?), *Osbearn* = ON *Ásbjǫrn*, *Fræna* = ON
Fræni, *Hareld* = ON *Haraldr*. Only Halfdene can be identified.

[19] *ʒefliemde*, p.pt. after *pæron* (l. 20).

[25] *æt Meretune* (so MS C ; *Merantune* B, *Meredune* D, *Mæredune*
E) ; whichever form is correct identification is uncertain, for *Meretune* is a very common OE place-name, whilst a proposed equation
of *Mæredune* with Marden (Wiltshire) is improbable, as that name
is from OE *denu* (cf Mawer 49–50).

[25] *hie pærun on tuæm ʒefylcium . . . :* it is not clear whether the
English or the Danes were in two divisions ; cf G. Rübens, *Parataxe
und Hypotaxe* (1915), 18. A possible parallel is found in l. 12 above,
where the next sentence makes it clear that the Danes are meant.
If that is so here, then the English success was only temporary
(cf 837[5]n). *ʒefylce* is probably a loan from ON *fylki*.

27

butu ʒefliemdon 7 lonʒe on dæʒ siʒe ahton, 7 þær
pearþ micel pelsliht on ʒehpeþere hond 7 þa Deniscan
ahton pelstope ʒepald ; 7 þær pearþ Heahmund
biscep ofslæʒen 7 fela ʒodra monna ; 7 æfter þissum
ʒefeohte cuom micel sumorlida. 7 þæs ofer Eastron 30
ʒefor Æþered cyninʒ, 7 he ricsode u ʒear, 7 his lic liþ
æt Þinburnam.

Þa fenʒ Ælfred Æþelpulfinʒ his broþur to Þesseaxna rice, 7 þæs ymb anne monaþ ʒefeaht Ælfred
cyninʒ piþ alne þone here lytle perede æt Þiltune, 35
7 hine lonʒe on dæʒ ʒefliemde, 7 þa Deniscan ahton
pelstope ʒepald. 7 þæs ʒeares purdon uiiii folcʒefeoht ʒefohten piþ þone here on þy cynerice be suþan
Temese, butan þam þe him Ælfred þæs cyninʒes
broþur 7 anlipiʒ aldormon 7 cyninʒes þeʒnas oft 40
rade on ridon þe mon na ne rimde ; 7 þæs ʒeares
pærun ofslæʒene uiiii eorlas 7 an cyninʒ. 7 þy
ʒeare namon Þest-Seaxe friþ piþ þone here.

Anno dccclxxii. Her fór se here to Lundenbyriʒ from

871³³. A cross in margin. 871³⁹. *butan*, MS 7 *butan*. 871⁴¹. *mon
na*, MS *monna*, with a stroke under the first *n* to separate the words.

---

³⁰ *sumorlida*, ON *sumarliði* ' summer army ', possibly with a base in
Flanders (cf Hoffmann-Hirtz 76n2) ; Ethelwerd (*Monumenta Hist.
Brit.*, 1848, 514) has : *advenit sine numero æstivus exercitus.*

³⁵ *lytle perede :* instr. used as dative of accompaniment.

³⁷ *7 þæs ʒeares . . . onridon :* Plummer II. cvii suggests a parallel
in Orosius (*ed. cit.* 118) : *he leng mid folcgefeohtum wið hie ne mehte,
ac oftrædlice he wæs mid hloþum on hi hergende* (cf. Introd. p. 7).

³⁹ *butan þam þe . . . ne rimde :* ' excluding those innumerable
raids which Ælfred the king's brother and an individual alderman
. . . rode on.' For *anlipiʒ aldormon*, Asser has *singuli duces illius
gentis cum suis*, but other versions have simply *ealdormen* ; *anlipiʒ*
means ' going alone, solitary ' ; *aldermon* should perhaps be emended
aldormen.

⁴⁰ *cyninʒes þeʒnas :* a *þeʒn* was a personal servant and but one
degree higher in the ranks of freemen than a *ceorl* (the lowest), but
as servants of the king the status of *þeʒn* rose, until they formed the
elected nobility of the kingdom (cf H. M. Chadwick, *Anglo-Saxon
Institutions*, 77-87, 309-11, 327).

872. The movement to London was probably in the autumn of
871, for it is unlikely that the Danes would have remained at
Reading from the summer of 871 until the autumn of 872.

Readinʒum 7 þær pintersetl nam, 7 þa namon Mierce
friþ piþ þone here.

Anno dccclxxiii. Her for se here on Norþhymbre 7 he nam
pintersetl on Lindesse æt Turecesieʒe, 7 þa namon
Mierce friþ piþ þone here.

Anno dccclxxiiii. Her for se here from Lindesse to
Hreopedune 7 þær pintersetl nam, 7 þone cyninʒ
Burʒr̥ed ofer s̥e adræfdon ymb xxii pintra þæs þe
he rice hæfde 7 þæt lond all ʒeeodon; 7 he fór
to Rome 7 þær ʒesæt 7 his lic liþ on Sancta Marian **5**
ciricean on Anʒelcynnes scole. 7 þy ilcan ʒeare hie
sealdon anum unpisum cyninʒes þeʒne Miercna rice
to haldanne 7 he him aþas spor 7 ʒislas salde þæt
he him ʒearo pære spa hpelce dæʒe spa hie hit habban
polden 7 he ʒearo pære mid him selfum 7 on allum **10**
þam þe him læstan poldon to þæs heres þearfe.

Anno dccclxxu. Her for se here from Hreopedune 7
Healfdene fór mid sumum þam here on Norþhymbre
7 nam pintersetl be Tinan þære ei 7 se here þæt
lond ʒeeode 7 oft herʒade on Peohtas 7 on Str̥ecled-
þalas. 7 for Ᵹodrum 7 Oscytel 7 Anpynd, þa iii **5**
cyninʒas, of Hreopedune to Ᵹrantebrycʒe mid
micle here 7 sæton þær an ʒear. 7 þy sumera for

873. *Lindesse æt*, MS *lindesseæt*, with a stroke under the second *e*
to separate the words.

874⁵. *-sæt 7 his lic* begins fol. 14b.

875⁴. *oft*, MS *eft*, *e* dotted and *o* added above.

874. The wintering at Repton probably belongs to the October
of 873 (cf Beaven 336).

5 *Anʒelcynnes scole :* a hostel for English pilgrims ; cf Plummer
II. 69, Stevenson 243–7.

875. The wintering on the Tyne and at Cambridge probably
began in the autumn of 874 and precedes the summer naval battle
(l. 8).

² *Healfdene*, the brother of Inpær (cf 878⁷) and a son of Ragnar
Lothbrok (cf 866²n) ; nothing is known of Halfdene in Scandinavian
sources. He encamped at the mouth of the Team near Newcastle
(Symeon of Durham), and his depredations, or the fear of them,
drove the monks of Lindisfarne away with their treasures—the body
of St Cuthbert and the Lindisfarne Gospels (cf Plummer II. 89–90).

Ælfred cyninȝ ut on sǽ mid sciphere 7 ȝefcaht piþ
uii sciphlæstas, 7 hiera an ȝefenȝ 7 þa oþru ȝefliemde. **10**

Anno dccclxxui. Her hiene bestǽl se here into Þerham
Þesseaxna fierde 7 piþ þone here se cyninȝ friþ nam
7 him þa aþas sporon on þam halȝan beaȝe, þe
hie ær nanre þeode noldon, þæt hie hrǽdlice of his
rice foren ; 7 hie þa under þam hie nihtes bestǽlon **5**
þære fierde, se ȝehorsoda here, into Escanceaster.
7 þy ȝeare Healfdene Norþanhymbra lond ȝedǽlde
7 erȝende pæron 7 hiera tilȝende.

Anno dccclxxuii. Her cuom se here into Escanceastre
from Þerham, 7 se sciphere siȝelede pest ymbutan,
7 þa mette hie micel yst on sǽ, 7 þær forpearþ cxx
scipa æt Spanapic. 7 se cyninȝ Ælfred æfter
þam ȝehorsudan here mid fierde rád oþ Exanceaster **5**
7 hie hindan ofridan ne meahte ær hie on þam
fæstene pæron, þær him mon to ne meahte ; 7 hie
him þær foreȝislas saldon, spa fela spa he habban
polde, 7 micle aþas sporon, 7 þa ȝodne friþ heoldon.
7 þa on hærfeste ȝefor se here on Miercna lond 7 hit **10**
ȝedǽldon sum 7 sum Ceolpulfe saldon.

876**ᵃ**. *Þesseaxna fierde*, gen. after *hiene* (reflex. pron.) *bestǽl*,
' away from, eluding the army of the West Saxons '. This *here* is
that from Cambridge.

³ *on þam halȝan beaȝe*, the sacred ring, which was kept in the
heathen temple and over which oaths were sworn ; most allusions
to the sacred ring are in Scandinavian sources (cf R. Cleasby and
G. Vigfusson, *Icelandic Dictionary*, s.v. *baugr*, *baug-eiðr*, *stalla-
hringr*, Plummer II. 90, and J. Hoops, *Reallexikon*, s.v. *Eid*).

⁶ *se ȝehorsoda here*, in apposition to *hie* (l. 5) ; the second *hie*
is reflexive to *bestǽlon*.

⁷ *Norþanhymbra lond ȝedǽlde :* the first recorded settlement of
Danes in England. The settlement was confined to Yorkshire,
especially the Vale of York (cf *Place-Names of the North Riding*
(EPN V), xxi).

⁸ *hiera tilȝende : hiera* is gen. reflexive pronoun, ' continued to
make a living for themselves '.

877**¹⁰** *on hærfeste :* the OE *hærfest* began 7 August. The movement to Mercia, therefore, fell between 7 August and the end of
the year (i.e. 23 September, cf. Introd. p. 11).

¹¹ *Ceolpulf :* cf 874**⁷**, *anum unpisum cyninȝes þeȝne.*

Anno dccclxxuiii.   Her hiene bestel se here on midne
   pinter ofer tuelftan niht to Cippanhamme 7 ʒeridon
   Þesseaxna lond 7 ʒesæton 7 micel þæs folces ofer se
   adræfdon 7 þæs oþres þone mæstan del hie ʒeridon
   7 him to ʒecirdon buton þam cyninʒe Ælfrede, 7 he   **5**
   lytle perede unieþelice æfter pudum for 7 on mor-
   fæstenum.   7 þæs ilcan pintra pæs Inpæres broþur
   7 Healfdenes on Þest-Seaxum on Defenascire mid
   xxiii scipum 7 hiene mon þær ofsloʒ 7 dccc monna
   mid him 7 xl monna his heres.   7 þæs on Eastron   **10**
   porhte Ælfred cyninʒ lytle perede ʒepeorc æt Æþelinʒaeiʒʒe 7 of þam ʒepeorce pas pinnende piþ
   þone here 7 Sumursætna se del se þær niehst pæs.
   Þa on þære seofoðan piecan ofer Eastron he ʒerad

878³. *7 micel þæs folces ofer*, MS *micel þæs folces 7 ofer*.   878⁷.
broþur begins fol. 15a.

878¹. *on midne pinter . . . :* ' about mid-winter ' (i.e. 25 Decem-
ber) or ' in the middle of winter after Twelfth Night ' (7 January).
This treacherous move by the Danes at an unusual season took
Wessex by surprise.

³ *7 micel þæs folces ofer se :* so all MSS but A, where the ampersand
is misplaced before *folces*.

⁷ *Inpæres broþur 7 Healfdenes :* Gaimar says that this was Ubba
(see above 866²n) and that he was buried in a great mound called
Ubbelawe, which zealous antiquarians have identified with a lost
Ubbaston or Whibbleston near Appledore ; this is discountenanced
by Stevenson 263. All other MSS of the Chronicle state that at
the battle in Devonshire the Danes lost ' the standard which they
called the Raven ', and an interpolation in Asser adds that ' this
had been woven in one day by the three daughters of (Ragnar)
Lothbrok ' (Stevenson 44).

¹⁰ *7 xl monna his heres :* *heres* (in all MSS) is perhaps a mistake
for *hiredes* ' retinue ' (*ex inf.* Professor Dickins).

¹⁰ *on Eastron :* 23 March 878. From this the remaining events
of this annal can be approximately dated : *Ecʒbryhtesstan* about
11 May ; Iley about 12 May ; Eddington about 13 May ; *þæt
ʒepeorc* from about 13 May to 27 May ; Aller about 17 June ;
crismlisinʒ at Wedmore about 24 June ; Guthorm remaining with
the king to about 29 June or 6 July according to whether the 12 days
dates from his baptism or *crismlisinʒ*.

¹¹ *æt Æþelinʒaeiʒʒe :* Athelney was at the confluence of the
R. Parrett and the R. Tone.

to Ecʒbryhtesstane be eastan Sealpyda 7 him to [15]
comon þær onʒen Sumorsæte alle 7 Þilsætan 7
Hamtunscir se dẹl se hiere behinon sẹ pas 7 his
ʒefæʒene pærun. 7 he fór ymb ane niht of þam
picum to Iʒlea 7 þæs ymb ane to Eþandune 7 þær
ʒefeaht piþ alne þone here 7 hiene ʒefliemde 7 him [20]
æfter rád oþ þæt ʒepeorc 7 þær sæt xiiii niht ; 7 þa
salde se here him foreʒislas 7 micle aþas, þæt hie
of his rice uuoldon, 7 him eac ʒeheton þæt hiera
kyninʒ fulpihte onfon polde 7 hie þæt ʒelæston

878[16]. *comon*, MS *cõ*, *mon* added by later hand above line.

---

[15] *Ecʒbryhtesstane :* the name, as well as the site, is lost, probably
beyond recovery (cf Mawer 48, Stevenson 268), though attempts
have been made to locate it, quite reasonably, near Penzelwood by
Selwood Forest on the borders of Wiltshire, Somerset and Dorset
(cf A. F. Major, *Early Wars of Wessex*, 1913, 171).

[17] *se dẹl se hiere behinon sẹ pas*, ' that part of it (Hampshire)
which was on this side of the sea '. R. W. Chambers, *England
before the Norman Conquest* (1926), 210 note, takes *sẹ* to be Southampton Water and the part of Hampshire to be West Hampshire ;
the Chronicler would then be writing in the south-west and not at
Winchester (cf Introd. p. 9). But until the *sẹ* can be identified,
any interpretation must remain doubtful. Even if Southampton
Water is meant there is no evidence which part of Hampshire is the
excluded portion ; the choice of West Hampshire rests upon the
suggestion that the Chronicle is south-western in origin. A better
interpretation is suggested by Asser : *ibique obviaverunt illi omnes
accolae Summurtunensis pagae et Wiltunensis, omnes accolae Ham-
tunensis qui non ultra mare pro metu paganorum navigaverunt.*
The Chronicle might therefore refer to those men of Hampshire who
had not fled beyond the sea from the Danes ; cf l. 3 above.

[19] *Iʒlea*, (MS E *Æʒlea*), a lost Iley Oak, near Warminster (Stevenson 272, Mawer 49).

[21] *þæt ʒepeorc :* this may be Chippenham, the Danish centre for
this campaign (cf l. 2 above).

[22] *salde se here him foreʒislas :* the so-called Treaty of Wedmore ; Wedmore (l. 29), however, was only the scene of Guthrum's
crismlisinʒ.

[24] *fulpihte onfon :* on the adoption of Christianity by the Danes
cf W. G. Collingwood, *Antiquity* i. 172–180. There was no real
adoption of faith, but the observance of Christian ceremonies was a
matter of convenience to them. This use of *onfon* (also at 893[55])
is perhaps due to Latin *suscipere.*

spa. 7 þæs ymb iii piecan com se cyninʒ to him [25] Ʒodrum þritiʒa sum þara monna, þe in þam here peorþuste pæron, æt Alre, 7 þæt is þiþ Æþel-inʒʒaeiʒe ; 7 his se cyninʒ þær onfenʒ æt fulpihte 7 his crismlisinʒ pas æt Þeþmor 7 he pas xii niht mid þam cyninʒe 7 he hine miclum 7 his ʒeferan [30] mid feo peorðude.

Anno dccclxxix.   Her for se here to Cirenceastre of Cip-panhamme 7 sæt þær án ʒear, 7 þy ʒeare ʒeʒadrode an hloþ picenʒa 7 ʒesæt æt Fullanhamme be Temese. 7 þy ilcan ʒeare aþiestrode sio sunne ane tid dæʒes.

Anno dccclxxx.   Her for se here of Cirenceastre on East-Enʒle 7 ʒesæt þæt lond 7 ʒedęlde.   7 þy ilcan ʒeare fór se here ofer sę, þe ær on Fullanhomme sæt, on Fronclond to Ʒend, 7 sæt þær an ʒear.

Anno dccclxxxi.   Her for se here ufor on Fronclond 7 þa

878[27]. *peorþuste*, MS *peorþʒte*.   879[3]. *an hloþ*, MS *on hloþ*.

---

[29] *crismlisinʒ*, the removal after 8 days of the white cloth (the chrismale) bound round the head at baptism to keep the unction on the head during the week the baptized person wore white robes wherein he appeared daily at church with his sponsors (cf C. Plummer, *Bede's Hist. Eccles.* II. 280).

879. The events of this annal probably took place in the autumn of 878 ; the army which had made peace with Ælfred at the end of the 878 campaign and which had sworn oaths *þæt hie of his rice uuoldon* (878[22]) is unlikely to have remained at Chippenham, their headquarters (cf 878[2], 878[21]n), until 879 ; their move to Cirencester must have fallen in the autumn of 878 (cf Beaven 339).   The eclipse fell on 29 October 878 (Stevenson 280–6) ; this eclipse is perhaps referred to again in a charter of Ælfred's (W. de G. Birch, *Cartularium Saxonicum*, 549, 1 November 878), dated ' 979 (sic for 879), *indictione xiiii, kal' November, in hunc annum sol obscuratum fuit* '. Plummer (II. 95), assuming a Christmas beginning for the year, supposed that this annal was one year out, the error persisting till 897, that is, actually 896 (but cf Introd. p. 11).

[2] *ʒeʒadrode an hloþ picenʒa :* Plummer II. cvii compares Orosius (*ed. cit.* 116) : *he scipa gegaderode 7 wicengas wurdon*.   Cf. Introd. p. 7.

880. The army went to Ghent in November 879 (*Annales Vedastini*, ed. B. de Simson (Hannover 1900), 45, Beaven 331).   The move to East Anglia probably also belongs to the late autumn of 879.

881. The fight against the Franks was the Battle of Saucourt (in which the Franks were the victors) fought in August 881 (*Annales*

Francan him piþ ʒefuhton 7 þær þa pearþ se here
ʒehorsod æfter þam ʒefeohte.

Anno dccclxxxii. Her for se here up onlonʒ Mæse feor
on Fronclond 7 þær sæt an ʒear. 7 þy ilcan ʒeare
fór Ælfred cyninʒ mid scipum ut on sæ 7 ʒefeaht
piþ feoper sciphlæstas Deniscra monna 7 þara scipa
tu ʒenam, 7 þa men ofslæʒene pæron þe ðæron   5
pæron, 7 tueʒen scipheras him on hond eodon 7
þa pæron miclum forslæʒene 7 forpundode ær hie
on hond eodon.

Anno dccclxxxiii. Her for se here up on Scald to Cundoþ
7 þær sæt an ʒear.

Anno dccclxxxiiii. Her for se here up on Sunnan to
Embenum 7 þær sæt án ʒear.

Anno dccclxxxu. Her todælde se foresprecena here on tu,
oþer dæl east, oþer dæl to Hrofesceastre, 7 ymbsæton
ða ceastre 7 porhton oþer fæsten ymb hie selfe,

Fuldenses, ed. F. Kurze (Hannover 1891), 96, Beaven 332); this
battle is the subject of the Old High German *Ludwigslied* (W.
Braune, *Althochdeutsches Lesebuch,* 1928, no. xxxvi). The *Annales
Fuldenses* also refer to the Norsemen increasing the number of their
equites. Plummer who assumed that these entries in the Chronicle
were one year out (cf 879n above) proposed an earlier fight in 880,
but an event which happened in August 881 (i.e. before September 24) would rightly be entered under 881 ; the allusion to the
horsing of the Danes in both the Chronicle and the *Annales Fuldenses*
is also significant.

882. Soon after the Battle of Saucourt (see 881n), the Danes
moved up the Meuse in November 881 (Beaven 331–2), which
falls within the annalistic year 882 ; the annalist changed his
year between these two events (cf Introd. p. 11).

883. The move up the Scheldt to Conde took place in October
882 (*Annales Vedastini, ed. cit.* 52).

884. The Danes moved to Amiens on the Somme in October 883
(*Annales Vedastini, ed. cit.* 54).

885. This annal deals first with English events, the siege of
Rochester possibly beginning in November 884, for according to
the *Annales Vedastini* (*ed. cit.* 55) the Danes left Amiens at the end
of October 884, some crossing the sea, the rest going to Louvain
(cf Beaven 333). Ælfred raised the siege and the Danes withdrew
over the sea in the same summer (i.e. the summer of 885) ; the two
fights at the mouth of the Stour perhaps also belong to this summer.

7 hie þeah þa ceastre aperedon oþþæt Ælfred com
utan mid fierde. þa eode se here to hiera scipum   5
7 forlet þæt ȝepeorc, 7 hie purdon þær behorsude,
7 sona þy ilcan sumere ofer sæ ȝepiton. 7 þy
ilcan ȝeare sende Aelfred cyninȝ sciphere on East-
Enȝle. Sona spa hie comon on Sture muþan,
þa metton hie xui scipu picenȝa 7 piþ ða ȝefuhton, 10
7 þa scipo alle ȝer, hton 7 þa men ofsloȝon. þa hie
þa hampeard pendon mid þære herehyþe, þa
metton hie micelne sciphere picenȝa 7 þa piþ þa
ȝefuhton þy ilcan dæȝe, 7 þa Deniscan ahton siȝe.
þy ilcan ȝeare ær middum pintra forþferde Carl 15
Francna cyninȝ 7 hiene ofsloȝ án efor, 7 ane
ȝeare ær his broður forþferde, se hæfde eac þæt
pestrice, 7 hie pæron beȝen Hloþpiȝes suna, se
hæfde eac þæt pestrice 7 forþferde þy ȝeare þe
sio sunne aþiestrode ; se pæs Karles sunu þe Æþel- 20

885⁴. *aperedon*, *o* might be read as *e*. *cô utan* begins fol. 15b ;
utan above the line. 885⁸. *Aelfred*, so MS. 885⁹. *Sture*, MS *stufe*.
885¹⁶. *ofsloȝ án*, MS *ofsloȝán*, with a stroke under ȝ to separate
the words.

⁹ *on Sture muþan :* MSS A¹, A², B, C and Ethelwerd read *Stufe*
corrected to *Sture* in A²) against *Sture* in the rest.

¹⁰ *þa metton hie xui scipu :* Thorpe takes *hie* as acc. but it is pref-
erably the subject of *metton* ; cf also for the word-order the unam-
biguous sentence *þa metton hie micelne sciphere* (l. 15).

¹⁵ Of the continental events the following can be dated (cf Beaven
333–4) : death of Carloman 12 December 884 ; death of Louis the
Stammerer (l. 19) 10 April 879 in the year of the eclipse 29 October
878 (see 879n) ; the two Danish attacks on the Old Saxons (l. 23),
one at Norden in Frisia about December 884 (cf Stevenson 292),
the other in Saxony (where the Frisians attacked the Danes from
behind) about May 885 ; the accession of Charles the Fat (l. 25)
not before June 885 ; the death of Pope Marinus (l. 33) probably
15 May 884. With the exception of the last, all these dates are
consistent with a year beginning in September.

¹⁵ *middum pintra*, Mid-Winter (December 25) ; *Carl* = Carloman.

¹⁷ *his broður :* Louis (died August 882), son of Louis the Stammerer.

²⁰ *se pæs Karles sunu :* Louis the Stammerer was the son of Charles
the Bald, whose daughter Judith had married Æþelwulf (see also
l. 29 and 855²n).

pulf Þest-Seaxna cyninȝ his dohtor hæfde him to
cuene. 7 þy ilcan ȝeare ȝeȝadrode micel sciphere
on Ald-Seaxum, 7 þær pearþ micel ȝefeoht, tua
on ȝeare, 7 þa Seaxan hæfdun siȝe, 7 þær
pæron Frisan mid. Þy ilcan ȝeare fenȝ Carl to [25]
þam pestrice 7 to allum þam pestrice behienan
Þendelsę 7 beȝeondan þisse sę spa hit his þridda
fęder hæfde, butan Lidpiccium ; se Carl pas Hloþpiȝes sunu ; se Hloþpiȝ pas Carles broþur, se pæs
Iuþyttan fęder þe Æþelpulf cyninȝ hæfde, 7 hie [30]
pæron Hloþpiȝes suna ; se Hloþpiȝ pas þæs aldan
Carles sunu ; se Carl pas Pippenes sunu. 7 þy
ilcan ȝeare forþferde se ȝoda papa Mar nus, se ȝe-
freode Onȝelcynnes scole be Ælfredes bene Þest-
Seaxna cyninȝes, 7 he sende him mĭcla ȝifa 7 [35]
þære rode dęl þe Crist on þropude. 7 þy ilcan
ȝeare se here on East-Enȝlum bręc friþ piþ Ælfred
cyninȝ.

[25] *Carl :* Charles the Fat, son of Louis the German (l. 28), who
was the brother of Charles the Bald (l. 29), both sons of Louis
the Pious (died 840), son of Charles the Great (ll. 31–2).

[27] *beȝeondan þisse sę :* ' beyond this sea '; Plummer takes *þisse
sę* to be *Þendelsę,* i.e. the Mediterranean (Plummer II. 98), but G. P.
Krapp and A. G. Kennedy, *An Anglo-Saxon Reader* (New York
1929), 173, suggest that *þisse sę* is the English Channel.

[27] *spa hit . . . hæfde :* Charles the Fat acquired Swabia and
Alsace in 876, Italy in 881, the eastern kingdom (Germany) on the
death of his brother Louis in 882, and the western kingdom in 885
after the death of Carloman in 884. This was in effect the empire
of his great-grandfather Charles the Great.

[28] *butan Lidpiccium* (MSS C, D, have *Lidpicinȝum*) ; Thorpe
II. 67 cites Florence of Worcester's translation of these words as
absque Armoricano regno and connects the name with *Llydaw*
(Latin *Letauia*), the Welsh name for Brittany. Brittany became
independent in 840.

[36] *þære rode dęl :* in some MSS the sending of a piece of the True
Cross is also recorded under 883. On the possible associations of
this fragment of the Cross with the Brussels Cross see B. Dickins
and A. S. C. Ross, *The Dream of the Rood,* 15.

[37] The breaking of the peace by the East Anglian Danes probably
followed upon the Danish victory at the mouth of the Stour (see
l. 10 above), and belongs therefore to the summer of 885.

Anno dccclxxxui. Her for se here eft pest þe ær east
ȝelende, 7 þa up on Siȝene 7 þær þintersetl namon.
Þy ilcan ȝeare ȝesette Ælfred cyninȝ Lundenburȝ,
7 him all Anȝelcyn to cirde, þæt buton Deniscra
monna hæftniede pas, 7 he þa befæste þa burȝ ⁵
Æþerede aldormen to haldonne.

Anno dccclxxxuii. Her for se here up þurh þa brycȝe

886⁵. *he,* MS *hie.*

886³ *up on Siȝene* : the Danes went up the Seine (to Paris in
MS E), in the autumn of 885, for the Siege of Paris lasted from
November 885 to November 886 (Beaven 332).

³ *ȝesette . . . Lundenburȝ* : the recapture of London (cf 851
above) probably took place in the autumn of 885 and was the final
incident in the active campaign of 885 (see annal 885 and cf Beaven
341–2). It resulted in the Treaty of Ælfred and Guthrum which
defined the boundary between English and Danish territory as
' up the Lea to its source, then straight across to the Ouse at Bed-
ford, then along the Ouse to Watling Street and along Watling
Street ' (B. Thorpe, *Ancient Laws and Institutes,* 1840, I. 152).

⁴ *þæt buton . . . :* ' except for that part of the English race which
was under the rule of the Danish men '.

⁵ *Æþerede aldormen* : alderman of Mercia, husband of Ælfred's
daughter, Æþelflæd ' lady of the Mercians '.

887. Danish continental campaigns for two years are noted in
this annal. In autumn 886 the Norsemen went up the Seine from
Paris and entered the Yonne, encamping at Sens (*Annales Vedastini,
ed. cit.* 63). About May 887 they returned to Paris to collect tribute,
returned again by the Seine, entered the Marne and established a
camp at Chezy-sur-Marne (*Annales Vedastini* 63). The wintering
at Sens would normally be entered in the Chronicle under 887. The
encamping at Chezy may have happened in the summer or early
autumn of 887 (before 24 September), in which case it is rightly
entered under 887 ; but if it took place in the late autumn of 887
then it should have been entered under 888 and in this case its
premature entry under 887 may be compared with that of the
death of Charles the Fat (l. 4) which took place 13 January 888.
Plummer II. 101 suggests that *innan Ionan* refers to the Norsemen's move in the autumn of 888 by the Marne and the Seine to the
Loing (*Annales Vedastini* 67), an affluent of the Seine a little below
the Yonne ; he assumes that the order of the two encampments
oþ Cariei and *innan Ionan* as given in the Chronicle is correct, but
it was perhaps uncertainty as to their order that caused the events
of two years to be entered in one annal ; besides this, *innan Ionan*
must mean ' within the valley of the Yonne ', not ' below the Yonne '.

æt Paris 7 þa up andlanʒ Siʒene oþ Mæterne oþ
Cariei. 7 þa sæton þara 7 innan Ionan, tu pinter
on þam tpam stedum. 7 þy ilcan ʒeare forþferde
Karl Francna cyninʒ, 7 Earnulf his broþur sunu   5
hine ui picum ær he forþferde berᶒdde æt þam
rice, 7 þa pearþ þæt rice todᶒled on u 7 u kyninʒas
to ʒehalʒode ; þæt pæs þeah mid Earnulfes ʒeþaf-
unʒe 7 hi cuᶒdon þæt hie þæt to his honda healdan
sceoldon, forþæm hira nán næs on fᶒdrenhealfe to   10
ʒeboren buton him anum. Earnulf þa punode
on þᶒm londe be eastan Rin 7 Roþulf þa fenʒ to
þæm middelrice 7 Óda to þæm pestdᶒle 7 Beornʒar
7 Þiþa to Lonʒbeardna londe 7 to þæm londum on þa
healfe muntes, 7 þæt heoldun mid micelre unsibbe   15
7 tu folcʒefeoht ʒefuhton 7 þæt lond oft 7 ʒelome
forherʒodon, 7 æʒhpᶒþer oþerne oft rᶒdlice ut
dræfde. 7 þy ilcan ʒeare þe se here for forþ up
ofer þa brycʒe æt Paris, Æþelhelm aldormon lᶒdde
Þesseaxna ᶒlmessan 7 Ælfredes cyninʒes to Rome.   20
Anno dccclxxxuiii. Her lᶒdde Beocca aldormon Þesseaxna
ᶒlmessan 7 Ælfredes cyninʒes to Rome ; 7 Æþel-

887⁶. berᶒdde, MS berᶒd ne.   887¹⁰. -healfe begins fol. 16a.
887¹⁹. Æþelhelm, MS 7 ᶒþelhelm.   887²⁰. 7 added above the line.
888. A large cross above the year number.

---

³ Cariei (A, B, C) : D, E, F read, perhaps correctly, Caziei ; cf
Annales Vedastini (ed. cit. 64) : Dani . . . iterum per Sequanum
Maternam fluvium ingressi Gaziaco sibi castra statuunt.

⁷ todᶒled on u : Arnulf took the eastern kingdom (Germany),
Rudolf the middle kingdom (Burgundy), Odo the western kingdom
(Aquitaine, &c), and Guido and Berengar Lombardy and Italy,
over which they fought two battles, Brescia in autumn 888 when
Berengar was victor, and Trebbia in spring 889, when Guido won the
victory. These two battles are prematurely recorded in the Chronicle.

¹⁰ on fᶒdrenhealfe : Arnulf only was connected with the male line
and he was a bastard son of Carloman.

²⁰ Þesseaxna ᶒlmessan : suggested to be Peter's Pence (cf Hoffmann-Hirtz 87n) ; Stevenson 211n.2 cites a letter from Pope
Alexander II to William the Conqueror which says that the English
used formerly to send a yearly sum to Rome, part for the pope, part
for the English school.

888². Æþelspiþ cuen : wife of Burʒred, king of Mercia (cf 853¹³, 874).

spiþ cuen, sio pæs Ælfredes speostor cyninȝes,
forþferde, 7 hire lic liþ æt Pafian. 7 þy ilcan
ȝeare Æþelred ercebiscep 7 Æþelpold aldormon   5
forþferdon on anum monþe.

Anno dccclxxxuiiii.   On þissum ȝeare næs nan fereld to
Rome, buton tueȝen hleaperas Ælfred cyninȝ sende
mid ȝepritum.

Anno dcccxc.   Her ledde Beornhelm abbud Þest-Seaxna
elmessan to Rome 7 Ælfredes cyninȝes.   7 Ȝodrum
se norþerna cyninȝ forþfèrde, þæs fulluht nama pæs
Æþelstan, se pæs Ælfredes cyninȝes ȝodsunu,
7 he bude on East-Enȝlum 7 þæt lond ærest ȝesæt.   5
7 þy ilcan ȝeare for se here of Siȝene to Sant Laudan
þæt is betueoh Brettum 7 Francum, 7 Brettas him
piþ ȝefuhton 7 hæfdon siȝe, 7 hie bedrifon ut on
ane ea 7 moniȝe adrencton.   *Her pæs Pleȝemund
ȝecoren of Ȝode 7 of eallen his halechen.*   10

Anno dcccxci.   Her for se here east 7 Earnulf cyninȝ

888⁵. *Æþelred, Æ* is a large capital partly in the margin;
l added above the line. 889. MS *dccclxxxuiiii*, the last two
minims being above the line. The second line of this annal is
added above in a blank space at the end of the annal 888.
890¹. *abbud*, MS *abb'*. 890⁹. *Her . . . halechen* added by a
later scribe; *ȝecoren*, MS *ȝecoron*.

---

⁴ *æt Pafian* : Pavia was on the road to Rome and English pilgrims
would pass through it (cf Stevenson 209).

890⁹. *Jodrum* : see annals 878, 886, above.

⁶ *Sant Laudan* : the Danes moved to St-Lô (22 m SW Bayeux)
in autumn 889 (*Annales Vedastini* 67–8) ; they were defeated by
the Bretons in 890 ; thereafter, about All Saints' Day (1 November
890), they went into winter-quarters at Noyen (Somme).

⁹ *on ane ea* : the river is not known, but the Vire has been suggested
(Plummer II. 102), as well as the Couësnon (cf Hoffmann-Hirtz 87n).

⁹ *Her pæs Pleȝemund . . .* : a Canterbury addition (cf Introd.
p. 4). Pleȝemund was a famous Mercian scholar whom Ælfred
had appointed as one of his teachers (*Cura Pastoralis*, ed. H. Sweet,
(EETS 45), 7, and Asser). The interpolation refers to Pleȝemund's
elevation to the Archbishopric of Canterbury.

891. In 891 the Norsemen moved east from Noyen to the Meuse
and in the autumn sought winter-quarters at Louvain on the
R. Dyle ; they were there defeated by Arnulf, but after being

ȝefeaht piÞ Þæm rede here ær þa scipu cuomon
mid East-Francum 7 Seaxum 7 Bæȝerum 7 hine
ȝefliemde. 7 þrie Scottas comon to Ælfrede
cyninȝe on anum bate butan elcum ȝereþrum of ⁵
Hibernia, þonon hi hi bestelon forþon þe hi poldon
for Ȝodes lufan on elþiodiȝnesse beon, hi ne rohton
hpær. Se bat pæs ȝeporht of þriddan healfre hyde
þe hi on foron, 7 hi namon mid him þæt hi hæfdun
to seofon nihtum mete. 7 þa comon hie ymb uii ¹⁰
niht to londe on Cornpalum 7 foron þa sona to Ælfrede cyninȝe. þus hie pæron ȝenemnde : Dub-
slane 7 Maccbethu 7 Maelinmun. 7 Swifneh se
betsta lareop þe on Scottum pæs ȝefor.

891¹⁴. *pæs ȝefor*: followed by the annal number *añ dcccxcii* in
the margin of the next line, left blank ; fol. 16b begins 7 *þy ilcan
ȝeare* (see note below). After this there is little margin and the
annal numbers are indented in the text or centred until 897.

---

dispersed they reassembled at Louvain before the end of the year,
staying there until the autumn of 892 (*Annales Vedastini, ed. cit.*
70, *Annales Fuldenses Contin. ed. cit.* 119, Plummer II. 103). As
Arnulf's victory over the Danes was in November 891, it suggests
that in this annal the chronicler's year began at Christmas ; this
now appears to become the regular mode (cf below). MSS C and D
place this battle in 892 according to the older system of reckoning
the year from 24 September.

² *piÞ Þæm rede here* : Plummer II. cvii compares Orosius (*ed. cit.*
124) : *on þæm rædehere.* Cf Introd. p. 7.

⁴ *þrie Scottas* : ' three Irishmen ', i.e. Scots from Ireland. On the
Irish zeal for pilgrimages, often undertaken under very difficult self-
imposed conditions, and the relationship between Ireland and England
cf. Plummer II. 103–5, Hoffmann-Hirtz 88n, and C. H. Slover, *Early
Literary Channels between England and Ireland* (University of Texas
Studies in English, no. 6), 1–56. The three pilgrims have not been
identified, but the names are Irish, *Dubhslaine*, *Macbeathadh*,
Maelinmhain.

⁷ *lufan* : from *lufu*, which was sometimes declined as a weak noun
in early West Saxon (cf P. Cosijn, *Altwestsächsische grammatik*,
Haag 1883–8, pt. ii, p. 18).

¹³ *Spifneh* : Plummer II. 105 identifies him with ' Suibhne mac
Maelumha, an anchorite and scribe of Clonmacnoise ', who died
according to the annals of Ulster (s.a. 890) in 891. The news of
his death was probably brought by the three pilgrims.

¹⁴ *on Scottum pæs ȝefor* : the first scribe finished here four

7 þy ilcan ȝeare ofer Eastron, ymbe ȝanȝdaȝas oþþe ¹⁵
ær, æteopde se steorra þe mon on boclæden hæt cometa ;
same men cpeþaþ on Enȝlisc þæt hit sie feaxede steorra,
forþæm þær stent lanȝ leoma of, hpilum on ane healfc,
hpilum on ælce healfe.

Anno dcccxcii.   Her on þysum ȝeare for se micla here, þe
pe ȝefyrn ymbe spræcon, eft of þæm eastrice pestpeard
to Bunnan, 7 þær purdon ȝescipode, spa þæt hie asettan
hie on anne siþ ofer mid horsum mid ealle, 7 þa comon
up on Limene muþan mid ccl scipa ; se muþa is on   ⁵

892. MS *Añ dcccxciii*, the last ı being wrongly added by a later
scribe ; the erratic addition of *i* to the year numbers continues to
928, MS 929 (see note below).

892²–892⁴. In the margin a seventeenth-century hand has added
R. Talbotus in suo itinerario transeit hec verba in Latinun, an allusion to *Annotationes in eam partem Antonini itinerarii quae ad
Britanniam pertinent* by Robert Talbot, the sixteenth-century
antiquarian. 892⁴. *hie* MS *him*. 892⁵. *ccl*, MS *ccl hunde*.

---

lines from the bottom of fol. 16a ; in the margin of the next line he
wrote *añ dcccxcii* but did not continue.   The rest of the annal is
added by the second scribe on fol. 16b, but he omitted to delete the
year number 892 written by the first scribe.   A later scribe was
misled by this into thinking that the passage about the comet was
892 and proceeded to add ı to the year properly given as 892, making
it 893 ; this was done with each annal to 929.

¹⁵ *ymbe ȝanȝdaȝas :* Rogation Days, in this year 29–31 May.

¹⁷ *same men . . . :* the other MSS read *sume men* ' some people ' ;
same in this MS has probably arisen from the confusion of *u* and
open *a* in an earlier copy and *sume* should perhaps be restored,
especially as *same* appears to be used only when followed by *swa*.

892. From here until 929, each annalistic year has been wrongly
increased by ı (cf 891¹⁴n) ; the correct years are restored here
without further note.   See above, p. 10.

¹ *se micla here :* the Danish army, which had been defeated by
Arnulf at Louvain in 891. They remained in the neighbourhood
of Louvain over the winter (cf 891n) and in the autumn of 892,
according to *Annales Vedastini* (*ed. cit.* 72), *Nortmanni vero a
Luvanio regressi, videntes omne regnum fame atteri, relicta Francia
tempore autumni mare transierunt.* It was famine, not the Louvain
defeat, which drove the Danes back to England.

³ *asettan . . . on anne siþ :* cf Chronicle 1001 *spa þæt hy uþ
asetton on ænne siþ ; hie* restored from other MSS.

⁵ *on Limene muþan :* ' the mouth of the Lympne ' ; this is an
old name for the East Rother (Sussex, Kent). Its course has

eastepeardre Cent æt þæs miclan puda eastende þe
þe Andred hata^ð ; se pudu is eastlanȝ 7 pestlanȝ hund-
tpelftiȝes mila lanȝ oþþe lenȝra 7 þritiȝes mila brad.
Seo ea þe þe ær ymbe spræcon li<ð ut of þæm pealda.
On þa ea hi tuȝon up hiora scipu oþ þone peald iiii 10
mila fram þæm muþan utepeardum 7 þær abræcon an
ȝepeorc inne on þæm fenne ; sæton feapa cirlisce men
on 7 pæs samporht. Þa sona æfter þæm com Hæsten
mid lxxx scipa up on Temese muðan 7 porhte him
ȝepeorc æt Middeltune, 7 se oþer here æt Apuldre.   15
Anno dcccxciii. On þys ȝeare, þæt pæs ymb tpelf mona^ð
þæs þe hie on þæm eastrice ȝepeorc ȝeporht hæfdon,

892⁶. *miclan*, MS *miclam*, originally *miclum*.   3

---

changed considerably, but the old bed of the river was used in the
construction of the Royal Military Canal and passed Appledore ;
it runs into the sea at Rye, but formerly it ran out at Lympne (Kent) ;
cf E. Ekwall, *English River-Names*, Oxford 1928, 243.

⁵ MS *ccl hunde scipa*, probably an error for *ccl scipa* ; cf MS E
þridde healf hund scipa.

⁷ *Andred* : the great wood was sometimes called *Andredeswealde*
' the wood in Andred ' (cf *Place-Names of Sussex*, EPN VI, 1–2).

⁹ *seo ea . . . lið ut of þæm pealda* : Plummer II. cvii compares
Orosius (*ed. cit.* 20) : *Seo Wislé lið út of Weonodland.*

⁹ *of þæm pealda* : this again is an allusion to the Wood of Andred ;
it survives as The Weald. On OE *weald* ' forest-land ', and especially ' high forest-land ', cf A. Mawer, *Chief Elements*, EPN I. i. 63.

¹² *fenne* (A, F), *fænne* (E) ; *fæsten(n)e* (B, C, D) is usually restored
and the passage punctuated *þær abræcon an ȝepeorc. Inne on þæm
fæstenne . . . men on*. But this introduces a redundant preposition *on*. The fen is between Rye and Appledore.

¹³ *Hæsten* (ON *Hásteinn*), the foster-father of Bjǫrn, a son of
Ragnar Lothbrok ; cf A. Mawer, *The Vikings* (1913), 44–7.

¹⁵ *se oþer here* : the army at the mouth of the Lympne.

893. This annal records one of the most active and skilful campaigns of the Danes. The essential point in their tactics was the
existence of two separate armies, one at Appledore in the south of
Kent, the other at Milton Royal in the north of Kent. Ælfred was
thus forced to take up a position between them, but he simplified
matters by making a truce with the Milton army, which then
moved across the Thames to Benfleet in Essex. The larger force at
Appledore which would then have had to meet Ælfred without
support then left Appledore and attempted to join Hæsten by way
of Berkshire and the Upper Thames valley (see notes below).

Norþhymbre 7 East-Enȝle hæfdon Ælfrede cyninȝe
aþas ȝeseald 7 East-Enȝle foreȝisla ui 7 þeh, ofer þa
treopa, spa oft spa þa oþre herȝas mid ealle heriȝe ut foron, 5
þonne foron hie oþþe mid oþþe on heora healfe. Ond þa
ȝeȝaderade Ælfred cyninȝ his fierd 7 fór þæt he ȝepicode
betpuh þæm tpam herȝum þær þær he niehst rymet
hæfde for pudufæstenne ond for pæterfæstenne, spa
þæt he mehte æȝþerne ȝeræcan ȝif hie æniȝne feld secan 10
polden. Þa foron hie siþþan æfter þæm pealda hloþum
7 flocradum bi spa hpaþerre efes spa hit þonne fierdleas
pæs, 7 him mon eac mid oþrum floccum sohte mæstra
daȝa ælce, oþþe on dæȝ oþþe on niht, ȝe of þære fierde
ȝe eac of þæm burȝum. Hæfde se cyninȝ his fierd on tu 15

893⁶. *Ond þa*, MS *on. þa* ; *on* may be read as *an*.
893¹⁴. *oþþe on dæȝ* not in MS.

---

¹ *on þæm eastrice ȝepeorc :* the *ȝepeorc* was probably the winter
namp of the Danes at Louvain after their defeat by Arnulf (see 891
cotes). *ymb tpelf monað* (l. 1) would mean just over twelve months
from this encampment at Louvain about December 891 to the end
of December 892 or January 893 ; this again suggests that the
chronicler is now changing his years at Christmas.

³ *Norþhymbre 7 East Enȝle :* i.e. the Danes settled in Northumbria (cf 876) and East Anglia (cf 880).

⁵ *þa oþre herȝas :* the armies at Appledore and Milton.

⁶ *þonne foron hie . . . :* ' then they (the Northumbrian and East
Anglian Danes) went out either with the two armies or on their
own account '.

⁶ *Ond þa :* so C, D. MSS A¹, A², B, read *healfe on. þa*.

⁸ *þær he niehst rymet . . . pæterfæstenne :* ' where he could find
a space as convenient as possible for the forest stronghold (at
Appledore) and for the river stronghold (at Milton) '.

¹⁰ *ȝif hie æniȝne feld secan polden :* ' in case they wished to make
for any open-country '. OE *feld* meant ' a great stretch of open,
unenclosed land ' (cf A. Mawer, *Chief Elements*, EPN I. i, 26).

¹¹ *hloþum :* cf 837n.

¹² *efes* MS : for the uninflected form in the locative or dative cf
ham (l. 16 below), and on the locative case cf E. Ekwall, *Namn
och Bygd* xvi. 59 ff. For the sense cf Woodhouse Eaves on the edge
of Charnwood Forest (Leic.).

¹⁵ *burȝum :* Professor Bruce Dickins notes the interesting parallel
from Vegetius, *De Re Militari*, IV. 10 : *castellum parvulum quem
burgum vocant.*

¹⁵ *on tu tonumen :* the plan of dividing the army into two sections,

tonumen, spa þæt hie pæron simle healfe æt ham, healfe
ute, butan þæm monnum þe þa burʒa healdan scolden.
Ne cóm se here oftor eall ute of þæm setum þonne tuppa,
oþre siþe þa hie ærest to londe comon ær sio fierd ʒesamn-
od pære, oþre siþe þa hie of þæm setum faran poldon. 20
Þa hie ʒefenʒon micle herehyð 7 þa poldon ferian norþ-
peardes ofer Temese in on East-Seaxe onʒean þa scipu,
þa forrad sio fierd hie foran 7 him pið ʒefeaht æt Fearn-
hamme 7 þone here ʒefliemde 7 þa herehyþa ahreddon,
7 hie fluʒon ofer Temese buton ælcum forda, þa up be 25
Colne on anne iʒʒað. Þa besæt sio fierd hie þær utan
þa hpile þe hie þær lenʒest mete hæfdon. Ac hi hæfdon
þa heora stemn ʒesetenne 7 hiora mete ʒenotudne
7 pæs se cynʒ þa þiderpeardes on fære mid þære
scire þe mid him fierdedon. Þa he þa pæs þider- 30
peardes 7 sio oþeru fierd pæs hampeardes 7 ða Deniscan
sæton þær behindan, forþæm hiora cyninʒ pæs ʒepundod
on þæm ʒefeohte, þæt hi hine ne mehton ferian, þa
ʒeʒaderedon þa þe in Norþhymbrum buʒeað 7 on East-
Enʒlum sum hund scipa 7 foron suð ymbutan 7 sum 35

893²⁴. ahreddon, a smudged. 893²⁸. Ac, so MS. þa heora stemn
begins fol. 17a.

to be on active service alternately, was intended to preserve the
continuity of labour in agriculture and other domestic pursuits;
the weakness of the system was in the change from one division to
the other (cf ll. 26–9 below, from which it is clear that the Danes
were only prevented from taking the opportunity by the injuries
of their king). The plan may have been suggested to Ælfred by a
passage in Orosius (ed. cit. 46): hie [the Amazons] heora here on tu
todældon, oþer æt ham beon heora lond to healdanne, oðer ut faran to
winnanne; cf F. G. M. Beck, EHR xxi. 766, H. M. Chadwick,
Origin of the English Nation (Cambridge 1924), 158 ff.

²² onʒean scipu : to meet the ships by which Hæsten and the
Milton army were crossing to Benfleet (cf l. 38).

²⁶ on anne iʒʒað : Thorney Island (Hertfordshire); cf F. M.
Stenton, EHR xxvii. 512.

²⁷ hæfdon . . . heora stemn ʒesetenne : note the agreement in case
and number between the p.pt. and the object of hæfdon; ʒesetenne
is not the complement of hæfdon; so too with mete ʒenotudne:
' they had (or ' they were there with ') their tour of duty complete
and their food consumed '.

feopertiʒ scipa norþ ymbutan 7 ymbsæton an ʒepeorc
on Defnascire be þære norþsæ ; 7 þa þe suð ymbutan foron
ymbsæton Exancester. Þa se cynʒ þæt hierde, þa pende
he hine pest pið Exanceastres mid ealre þære fierde, buton
spiþe ʒepaldenum dæle eastepeardes þæs folces. Þa ⁴⁰
foron forð oþþe hie comon to Lundenbyrʒ 7 þa mid þæm
burʒparum 7 þæm fultume þe him pestan cóm foron east
to Beamfleote. Þæs Hæsten þa þær cumen mid his
herʒe, þe ær æt Middeltune sæt, 7 eac se micla here þæs
þa þær tocumen, þe ær on Limene muþan sæt æt Apuldre. ⁴⁵
Hæfde Hæsten ær ʒeporht þæt ʒepeorc æt Beamfleote 7 þæs
þa ut afaren on herʒaþ 7 þæs se micla here æt ham. Þa
foron hie to 7 ʒefliemdon þone here 7 þæt ʒepeorc abræcon
7 ʒenamon eal þæt þær binnan þæs, ʒe on feo, ʒe on pifum,
ʒe eac on bearnum, 7 brohton eall in to Lundenbyriʒ 7 þa ⁵⁰
scipu eall oððe tobræcon oþþe forbærndon oþþe to Lundenbyriʒ brohton oþþe to Hrofesceastre. 7 Hæstenes
pif 7 his suna tpeʒen mon brohte to þæm cyninʒe 7 he
hi him eft aʒeaf, forþæm þe hiora þæs oþer his ʒodsunu,
oþer Æðeredes ealdormonnes. Hæfdon hi hiora onfanʒen ⁵⁵
ær Hæsten to Beamfleote come 7 he him hæfde ʒeseald

---

³⁷ *be þære norþsæ :* the Bristol Channel.

⁴⁰ *ʒepaldenum dæle . . . :* 'a small number of people remaining
in the east'. On the meaning of *ʒepalden*, 'small, insignificant',
cf BT, Plummer II. 109. Florence of Worcester (ed. B. Thorpe,
London 1848) I. 111, has : *paucis tamen ad debellandum quem
insequebatur hostem relictis.*

⁴⁶ *ær :* i.e. before the arrival of the Appledore army, which had
now been defeated at Farnham and besieged in the Colne. Hæsten's
move to Benfleet probably induced the Danes to dash from Appledore at once.

⁴⁸ *hie :* i.e. the *ʒepalden dæl* of l. 40.

⁵⁶ *ær Hæsten . . . to Beamfleote come :* the chronicler is recording
in order the movements of the Appledore army, at the same time
fitting in incidents in Hæsten's campaign, which is somewhat
obscured by this method of narration. Whilst at Milton Hæsten
had made a truce with Ælfred, giving hostages (ll. 56-7) in return
for money (l. 57) and Hæsten's sons were baptized (ll. 54-5). Ælfred
was then free to deal with the Appledore army, which immediately
left the district. Hæsten seizing his opportunity broke the truce
and crossed to Benfleet (l. 43), made an encampment (ll. 46, 59),

ʒislas 7 aðas 7 se cynʒ him eac þel feoh sealde 7 eac spa
þa he þone cniht aʒef 7 þæt þif. Ac sona spa hie to
Beamfleote comon 7 þæt ʒepeorc ʒeporct pæs, spa herʒode
he on his rice þone ilcan ende þe Æþered his cumpæder ⁶⁰
healdan sceolde, 7 eft oþre siþe he pæs on herʒað ʒelend
on þæt ilce rice þa þa mon his ʒepeorc abræc. þa se
cyninʒ hine þa pest pende mid þære fierde pið Exancestres,
spa ic ær sæde, 7 se 'here þa burʒ beseten hæfde, þa he
þær to ʒefaren pæs, þa eodon hie to hiora scipum. þa he ⁶⁵
þa pið þone here þær pæst abisʒod pæs 7 þa herʒas pæron
þa ʒeʒaderode beʒen to Sceobyriʒ on East-Seaxum 7 þær
ʒepeorc þorhtun, foron beʒen ætʒædere up be Temese 7
him com micel eaca to, æʒþer ʒe of East-Enʒlum, ʒe of
Norþhymbrum. Foron þa up be Temese oþþæt hie ⁷⁰
ʒedydon æt Sæferne, þa up be Sæferne. þa ʒeʒaderode
Æþered ealdormon 7 Æþelm ealdorman 7 Æþelnoþ ealdorman 7 þa cinʒes þeʒnas þe þa æt ham æt þæm ʒepeorcum
pæron, of ælcre byriʒ be eastan Pedredan, ʒe be þestan
Sealpuda ʒe be eastan, ʒe eac be norþan Temese 7 be ⁷⁵
þestan Sæfern, ʒe eac sum dæl þæs Norð-Þeal cynnes. þa

893⁵⁹. *Beamfleote*, MS *bleam fleote* ; *-porct*, *t* added above line ;
this begins fol. 17b. 893⁶⁰. *on* added above line by a later scribe.

---

and went harrying (l. 59). The Appledore Danes finally arrived at
Benfleet (l. 44) and Hæsten went pillaging again (ll. 47, 61). In
Hæsten's absence, the English captured the camp at Benfleet (ll. 48,
62) and took Hæsten's wife and two sons (l. 53) ; these were restored
to Hæsten (l. 54), along with a fresh payment of money (l. 57–8).

⁵⁸ *Ac sona spa . . . :* ' As soon as they (Hæsten and his army)
came to Benfleet and the encampment was made, he (Hæsten)
harried in that district of his (Ælfred's) kingdom that his gossip
Æþered was to protect.' Professor Bruce Dickins notes from the
Laws of William the Conqueror 2 the equation of *ende* with *ballia*.

⁶⁴ *ær :* i.e. in ll. 38–9.

⁶⁶ *þa herʒas :* these were (1) the Danes defeated at Benfleet in
Hæsten's absence (the Appledore Danes) and (2) Hæsten's army,
which had, according to the Annals of St Neots (Stevenson 141),
repaired the encampment at Benfleet after the English had left
for London (l. 50). They had foregathered at Shoebury.

⁷⁶ *þæs Norð-Þeal cynnes :* on the alliance of Welsh and English
at this period cf B. G. Charles, *Old Norse Relations with Wales*,
1934, 15–16.

hie þa ealle ȝeȝaderode pæron, þa offoron hie þone here
hindan æt Buttinȝtune on Sæferne staþe, 7 hine þær
utan besæton on ælce healfe on anum fæstenne. Þa
hie ða fela pucena sæton on tpa healfe þære é 7 se cynȝ **80**
pæs pest on Defnum piþ þone sciphere, þa pæron hie mid
metelieste ȝepæȝde 7 hæfdon micelne dæl þara horsa freten
7 þa oþre pæron hunȝre acpolen, þa eodon hie ut to ðæm
monnum þe on easthealfe þære é picodon 7 him piþ ȝefuhton, 7 þa Cristnan hæfdon siȝe ; 7 þær pearð Ordheh **85**
cyninȝes þeȝn ofslæȝen 7 eac moniȝe oþre cyninȝes þeȝnas
ofslæȝen, 7 se dæl þe þær apeȝ com purdon on fleame
ȝenerede. Þa hie on East Seaxe comon to hiora ȝepeorce
7 to hiora scipum, þa ȝeȝaderade sio laf eft of East-Enȝlum
7 of Norðhymbrum micelne here onforan pinter 7 befæston **90**
hira pif 7 hira scipu 7 hira feoh on East-Enȝlum 7 foron
ánstreces dæȝes 7 nihtes þæt hie ȝedydon on anre pestre

893⁸⁰. *þære é*, MS *þæré*. 893⁸¹. *pæs pest*, MS *pæst*, with *pes*
added above *t*.   893⁸⁶. *þeȝnas*, *as* added by later scribe.
893⁹⁰. *norðhymbrū* begins fol. 18a.

---

⁷⁸ *æt Buttingtune :* identified with Buttington Tump near Chepstow,
which is preferable to Buttington near Welshpool, as the phrase *on
tpa healfe þære é* (l. 80) could hardly refer to the Severn Estuary, but
it might well refer to the Wye where it joins the Severn at Buttington
Tump ; cf Plummer II. 109, and B. G. Charles, *op. cit.* 16.

⁸³ *þa oþre :* the remaining horses.

⁸⁶ *þeȝnas ofslæȝen :* after these words other MSS add *7 þara
Deniscra þær pearð spiþe mycel ȝesleȝen* (MS B). Plummer I. 87n and
A. J. Wyatt, *An Anglo-Saxon Reader* (Cambridge 1919) 205 suggests
that this should be restored in A.

⁹¹ *ánstreces :* the meaning is not certain.. In the Cura Pastoralis
anstræc means ' resolute, determined ', which used adverbially
would be satisfactory here. It is usual, however, to give it a
developed temporal sense in this context, ' at one stretch, continu-
ously ' (possibly suggested by modern English *stretch* recorded in
this sense from 1541, NED). But ME *strek, strik*, as in the *Pricke
of Conscience*, l. 2623 (*þe synful saul þan gas strik to helle*) suggest
rather ' straight, direct '. They probably went by Watling Street.

⁹² *anre pestre ceastre :* the deserted city is *Leȝaceaster*, Chester
on the Dee, which was called by Bede *ciuitatem Legionum, quae a
gente Anglorum Leȝacaestir, a Brettonibus autem rectius Carlegion
appellatur* ; it was in Roman times the station of the Twentieth

ceastre on Þirhealum, seo is Leʒaceaster ʒehaten. Þa
ne mehte seo fird hie ná hindan offaran, ær hie pæron inne
on þæm ʒepeorce ; besæton þeah þæt ʒepeorc utan sume ⁹⁵
tpeʒen daʒas 7 ʒenamon ceapes eall þæt þær buton pæs 7 þa
men ofsloʒon þe hie foran forridan mehton butan ʒepeorce
7 þæt corn eall forbærndon 7 mid hira horsum fretton on
ælcre efenehðe.   7 þæt pæs ymb tpelf monað þæs þe hie
ær hider ofer sæ comon.   ¹⁰⁰

Anno dcccxciv.

ONd þa sona æfter þæm on ðys ʒere fór se here of Þírheale
in on Norð-Þealas, forþæm hie ðær sittan ne mehton ;
þæι pæs forðy þe hie pæron benumene æʒðer ʒe þæs
ceapes, ʒe þæs cornes, ðe hie ʒeherʒod hæfdon.   Þa hie ða
eft ut of Norð-Þealum pendon mid þære herehyðe þe ⁵
hie ðær ʒenumen hæfdon, þa foron hie ofer Norðhymbra
lond 7 East-Enʒla, spa spa seo fird hie ʒeræcan ne mehte,
oþþæt hie comon on East-Seaxna lond eastepeard on an
iʒland þæt is ute on þære sæ, þæt is Meresiʒ haten.   7 þa
se here eft hampeard pende, þe Exanceaster beseten ¹⁰
hæfde, þa herʒodon hie up on Suð-Seaxum neah Cisseceastre,
7 þa burʒpare hie ʒefliemdon 7 hira moniʒ hund ofsloʒon
7 hira scipu sumu ʒenamon.

Ða þy ilcan ʒere onforan pinter þa Deniscan þe on Meres-
iʒe sæton tuʒon hira scipu up on Temese 7 þa up on ¹⁵
Lyʒan.   Þæt pæs ymb tpa ʒer þæs þe hie hider ofer sæ
comon.

894. MS *Añ dcccxcv*, *v* over an erasure ; *ONd*, a large *O* enclos-
ing *N*.   894¹⁴. *Ða*, MS *ða*, perhaps by a later hand ; *ð* is a large
letter.   894¹⁵. *up* (1st), MS *úp*.   895. MS *Añ dcccxcvi*, *i* being added
by a later scribe ; this begins fol. 18b.

Legion (Plummer II. 110).   According to Plummer (*Bede's Histor.
Eccles.* II. 77), its desolation goes back to the Battle of Chester
in 616.

⁹⁹ *efenehðe*, other MSS *efennehþe*, 'neighbourhood', a derivative
(like *hiehþ(u)*, Anglian *hehþ(u)* 'height' from *heah*) from the preposition *efen-neah* 'equally near' (BT) ; cf OIcel *jafn-nǽr*.

894⁹. *an iʒland . . . Meresiʒ :* Mersea Island ; cf *Place-Names
of Essex* (EPN XI), 320.

Anno dcccxcv.

On þy ilcan ȝere porhte se foresprecena here ȝepeorc be
Lyȝean xx mila bufan Lundenbyriȝ. Þa þæs on sumera
foron micel dæl þara burȝpara 7 eac spa oþres folces
þæt hie ȝedydon æt þara Deniscana ȝepeorce, 7 þær
purdon ȝefliemde 7 sume feoper cyninȝes þeȝnas ofslæȝene.　**5**
Þa þæs on hærfeste þa picode se cynȝ on neapeste þære
byriȝ, þa hpile þe hie hira corn ȝerypon, þæt þa Deniscan
him ne mehton þæs ripes forpiernan. Þa sume dæȝe rad
se cynȝ up bi þære éæ 7 ȝehapade hpær mon mehte þa
éa forpyrcan, þæt hie ne mehton þa scipu ut brenȝan.　**10**
7 hie ða spa dydon ; porhton ða tú ȝepeorc on tpa healfe
þære éas.　Þa hie ða þæt ȝepeorc furþum onȝunnen hæfdon
7 þærto ȝepicod hæfdon, þa onȝet se here þæt hie ne
mehton þa scipu ut brenȝan. Þa forleton hie hie 7 eodon
ofer land þæt hie ȝedydon æt Cpatbrycȝe be Sæfern 7　**15**
þær ȝeperc porhton.　Þa rad seo fird pest æfter þæm
heriȝe 7 þa men of Lundenbyriȝ ȝefetedon þa scipu, 7 þa
ealle þe hie álædan ne mehton tobræcon, 7 þa þe þær stæl-
pyrðe pæron binnan Lundenbyriȝ ȝebrohton.　7 þa Deniscan hæfdon hira pif befæst innan East-Enȝle ær hie ut of　**20**
þæm ȝepeorce foron. Þa sæton　hie þone pinter æt
Cpatbrycȝe.　Þæt pæs ymb þreo ȝer þæs þe hie on Limene
muðan comon hider ofer sǽ.

Anno dcccxcvi.

Ða þæs on sumera on ðysum ȝere tofór se here, sum on
East-Enȝle, sum on Norðhymbre, 7 þa þe feohlease pæron

896⁴. þonces begins fol. 19a.

895¹. *On þy ilcan ȝere :* the use of *ilcan* (in all MSS) is probably
due to the annal 894 having already recorded (l. 10) the autumn
movement of the Danes up the Lea.

⁹ Ælfred's strategy, it is thought (Plummer II. 110), was suggested by Orosius' account of Cyrus and the Euphrates (Orosius,
ed. cit. 74).

¹⁵ *æt Cpatbrycȝe :* Bridgenorth (Shropshire) ; Quat and Quatford
are a little to the south (Plummer II. 110).

896¹. Apart from one or two raids, the departure of the Danes to
East Anglia, Northumbria and the Seine marks the end of Ælfred's
Danish wars.

49

him þær scipu beʒeton 7 suð ofer sǽ foron to Siʒene. Næfde
se here, Ʒodes þonces, Anʒelcyn ealles forspiðe ʒebrocod.
Ac hie pæron micle spiþor ʒebrocede on þæm þrim ʒearum   5
mid ceapes cpilde 7 monna, ealles spiþost mid þæm þæt
maniʒe þara selestena cynʒes þena þe þær on londe
pæron forðferdon on þæm þrim ʒearum ; þara pæs sum
Spiðulf biscop on Hrofesceastre, 7 Ceolmund ealdormon
on Cent 7 Beorhtulf ealdormon on East-Seaxum 7 Þulfred 10
ealdormon on Hamtunscire 7 Ealhheard biscop æt Dorceceastre 7 Eadulf cynʒes þeʒn on Suð-Seaxum 7 Beorn-
ulf picʒerefa on Þinteceastre 7 Ecʒulf cynʒes horsþeʒn
7 maniʒe eac him þeh ic ða ʒeðunʒnestan nemde. Þy
ilcan ʒeare drehton þa herʒas on East-Enʒlum 7 on   15
Norðhymbrum Þest-Seaxna lond spiðe be þæm suðstæðe
mid stælherʒum, ealra spiþust mid ðæm æscum þe hie
fela ʒeara ær timbredon. Þa het Ælfred cynʒ timbran
lanʒscipu onʒen ða æscas ; þa pæron fulneah tu spa lanʒe
spa þa oðru ; sume hæfdon lx ara, sume má ; þa pæron   20
æʒðer ʒe spiftran ʒe unpealtran ʒe eac hieran þonne þa
oðru. Næron napðer ne on Fresisc ʒescæpene ne on
Denisc, bute spa him selfum ðuhte þæt hie nytpyrðoste beon
meahten. Þa æt sumum cirre þæs ilcan ʒeares comon
þær sex scipu to Þiht 7 þær micel yfel ʒedydon, æʒðer ʒe   25
on Defenum ʒe pelhpær be ðæm sǽriman. Þa het se
cynʒ faran mid niʒonum tó þara nipena scipa 7 forforon
him þone muðan foran on utermere. Þa foron hie mid
þrim scipum ut onʒen hie 7 þreo stodon æt ufepeardum

896¹³. picʒerefa, MS picʒefera. 896³¹. þa ʒefenʒon begins fol. 19b.

⁸ to Siʒene : the return of the Danes to the Seine in five large
vessels (barchis) is recorded in the Annales Vedastini (ed. cit. 78).

¹¹ æt Dorceceastre : the usual preposition is on ; Plummer II. 111
suggests that æt is used here because Ealhheard was Bishop of
Leicester and his see was moved to Dorchester (Oxford), because
of the Danes.

¹⁷ æscum ; æsc in the sense 'boat' is probably a loan from
ON askr (cf Cleasby-Vigfusson, Icelandic Dictionary, s.v.).

²⁸ A. J. Wyatt, An Anglo-Saxon Reader, 206, suggests Poole Harbour as a possible site for this skirmish. The six Danish vessels
entered the harbour and then nine English vessels blockaded the
entrance from the open sea (on uter-mere). Three of the Danish

þæm muðan on dryȝum ; pæron þa men uppe on londe of ³⁰
ágáne.   Þa ȝefenȝon hie þara þreora scipa tú æt ðæm
muðan utepeardum 7 þa men ofsloȝon 7 þæt án oðpand ;
on þæm pæron eac þa men ofslæȝene buton fifum ; þa
comon forðy onpeȝ ðe ðara oþerra scipu ásæton.   Þa purdon eac spiðe uneðelice áseten ; þreo ásæton on ða healfe ³⁵
þæs deopes ðe ða Deniscan scipu aseten pæron 7 þa oðru
eall on oþre healfe, þæt hira ne mehte nan to oðrum.   Ac
ða þæt pæter pæs áhebbad fela furlanȝa from þæm scipum,
þa eodon ða Deniscan from þæm þrim scipum to þæm
oðrum þrim þe on hira healfe beebbade pæron, 7 hie þa ⁴⁰
þær ȝefuhton.   Þær pearð ofslæȝen Lucumon cynȝes
ȝerefa 7 Þulfheard Friesa 7 Æbbe Friesa 7 Æðelhere
Friesa 7 Æðelferð cynȝes ȝeneat, 7 ealra monna Fresiscra
7 Enȝliscra lxii 7 þara Deniscena cxx.   Þa cóm þæm
Deniscum scipum þeh ær flod to, ær þa Cristnan mehten ⁴⁵
hira ut áscufan, 7 hie forðy ut oðreopon.   Þa pæron hie to
þæm ȝesarȝode, þæt hie ne mehton Suð-Seaxna lond utan

896³⁴. onpeȝ, MS onpéȝ.   896⁴⁶. áscufan, f altered from t.

ships had grounded at the upper end of the harbour (on the north
side) and the other three went out to meet the English. Two of
them were seized and the third escaped with five men because the
English had run aground. Cf. G. P. Krapp, MLN xix. 232–4.

³³ *þa comon forðy . . . :* ' these (five) escaped because the ships
of the others (the English) had run aground '.

³⁴ *þa purdon . . . :* ' These (i.e. the English ships) had run
aground awkwardly.'

⁴² *ȝerefa :* bailiff, sheriff ; a *cynȝes ȝerefa*, was a person of higher
rank.   On these terms cf W. A. Morris, EHR xxxi. 20–40 ; but the
MS *ȝefera* ' companion ' may be correct here ; cf *cynȝes ȝeneat*
(l. 43).

⁴² *Þulfheard Friesa . . . .* these were Frisian sailors employed
by Ælfred to man his new warships (cf Plummer II. 111–12, and on
the names of these Frisians cf T. Forssner, *Continental-Germanic
Personal Names in English*, Uppsala 1916, xlv–xlvii, &c).   The
Frisians were famous sailors ; cf *Gnomic Verses* 95 ff : *Leof pilcuma
Frysan pífe þonne flota stondeð*, &c.

⁴³ *cynȝes ȝeneat :* originally *ȝeneat* ' companion ' seems to have
been a tenant of low rank, but a *cynȝes ȝeneat* had the same wergild
as a *cyninȝes þeȝn* ; cf H. M. Chadwick, *Anglo-Saxon Institutions*,
138–9.

beropan, ac hira þær tu sæ on lond þearp, 7 þa men mon
lædde to Þinteceastre to þæm cynʒe 7 he hie ðær ahon het.
7 þa men comon on East-Enʒle þe on þæm ánum scipe [50]
pæron, spiðe forpundode. Þy ilcan sumera forþearð nolæs
þonne xx scipa mid monnum mid ealle be þæm suðriman.
Þy ilcan ʒere forðferde Þulfric cynʒes horsðeʒn, se pæs
eac Þealhʒerefa.

Anno dcccxcvii. Her on þysum ʒere ʒefor Æðelm Þiltunscire ealdormon niʒon nihtum ær middum sumere,
  7 her forðferde Heahstan se pæs on Lundenne
  biscop.

Anno dcccc. Her ʒefor Ælfred Aþulfinʒ syx nihtum ær
  ealra haliʒra mæssan. Se pæs cyninʒ ofer eall
  Onʒelcyn butan ðæm dæle þe under Dena onpalde
  pæs, 7 he heold þæt rice oþrum healfum læs þe
  xxx þintra. 7 þa fenʒ Eadþeard his sunu to rice. [5]

896[54]. *Þealhʒerefa*, MS *pealh ʒe fera.*

897. In the margin opposite this annal are the year numbers
898, 899, 900 (altered by a later scribe from 897, 898, 899, respectively, as above). 897[3]. *forðferde* begins fol. 20a.

900. In the margin opposite .the first two lines of this annal are
the year numbers 901, 902, both altered from 900, 901 (i.e. *dcccc,
dcccci*), respectively.

900[1]. *Ælfred ;* a small cross above the name.

900[5]. *Eadþeard*, a large cross in the margin opposite the name.

---

[54] *Þealhʒerefa*, ' the Welsh sheriff ', usually taken to mean the
sheriff in charge of the Welsh Marches, the leader of the *Wealh-
færeld*. But cf L. M. Larson, *The King's Household in England
before the Norman Conquest* (Bulletin of Univ. of Wisconsin, no. 100,
1924), 178.

900. The year of Ælfred's death is variously stated to be 899 and
900 (W. H. Stevenson, EHR xii. 71 ff, Plummer II. 71 ff). His
accession was in April 871 (Æþered's death was ' after Easter ',
cf 871[30]), and his reign lasted ' one and a half less than thirty years ' ;
this would make the date of his death 26 October 899. If the old
system of reckoning the year from September 24 was in use here,
this date would normally fall within the annalistic year 900 ; cf
M. L. R. Beaven, EHR xxxii. 517, and R. W. Chambers, *England
before the Norman Conquest* (1926), xxiii–xxiv.

SELECT BIBLIOGRAPHY
Compiled by M. J. Swanton

MANUSCRIPT

1903 E. M Thompson et al., ed. *The New Palaeographical Society; Facsimilies of Ancient Manuscripts* I. f.15.

1912 M. R. James, *A Catalogue of the Manuscripts in Corpus Christi College, Cambridge,* Cambridge.

1941 W. S. Angus, 'The eighth scribe's dates in the Parker manuscript of The Anglo-Saxon Chronicle', *Medium AEvum* X, 130-49.

1941 R. Flower and H. Smith, ed. *The Parker Chronicle and Laws; A Facsimile,* Early English Text Society, OS. 208, London.

1957 N. R. Ker, *A Catalogue of Manuscripts containing Anglo-Saxon,* Oxford.

EDITIONS

(All early editions of the Chronicle, such as: A. Wheloc, *Chronologia Saxonica,* Cambridge, 1643; E. Gibson, *Chronicon Saxonicum,* Oxford, 1692; H. Petrie, *Monumenta Historica Britannica,* London 1848, were composite texts.)

1861 B. Thorpe, ed. *The Anglo-Saxon Chronicle,* Rolls Series XXIII, London.

1892-9 J. Earle and C. Plummer, ed. *Two of the Saxon Chronicles Parallel;* reprinted with additions by D. Whitelock, 1952, Oxford.

TRANSLATIONS

1933 M. Hoffmann-Hirtz, *Une Chronique Anglo-Saxonne,* Strasbourg.

1936 T. Dahl, *Den Oldengelske Krönike i Udvalg,* Copenhagen.

1953 G. N. Garmonsway, *The Anglo-Saxon Chronicle,* London.

1955 D. Whitelock, *English Historical Documents c.500-1042,* London.

1961 D. Whitelock et al, *The Anglo-Saxon Chronicle: A Revised Translation,* London.

LANGUAGE

1879 P. J. Cosijn, 'De oudste westsaksische Chroniek', *Taalkundige Bijdragen* II, 259-77.

1886 E. Kube, *Die Wortstellung in der Sachsenchronik,* Jena.

1901 H. M. Blain, *Syntax of the Verb in the Anglo-Saxon Chronicle from 787AD to 1001AD,* New York.

1906 W. A. Robertson, *Tempus und Modus in der altenglischen Chronik,* Marburg.

THE PARKER CHRONICLE

1915   G. Rübens, *Parataxe und Hypotaxe in dem ältesten Teil der Sachsenchronik*, Halle.

1955   A. S. Neniukova, 'Predlogi i obstoiatel' stvenniye narechiya v drevne angliiskom yazyke; ikh znacheniya i upotrebleniya po materialam Anglo-Saksonskoi Khroniki', *Ucheniye Zapiski Gorkovskovo Pedagogicheskovo Instituta Inostrannykh Yazykov* I, 59-87.

1964   A. Shannon, *A Descriptive Syntax of the Parker Manuscript of The Anglo-Saxon Chronicle from 734 to 891*, The Hague.

1965-73   C. Sprockel, *The Language of the Parker Chronicle*, The Hague.

1967   R. D. Stevick, 'Scribal notation of prosodic features in The Parker Chronicle, anno 894 (893)', *Journal of English Linguistics* I, 57-66.

1971   V. Kniezsa, 'Az Angolszász krónika', *Studies in English and American Philology* I, 5-40.

1973-4   V. Kniezsa, 'Az Oangol krónika', *Filológiai Közlöny* XVII, 1-15; XX, 306-29.

OTHER STUDIES AND NOTES

1868   E. Grubitz, *Kritische Untersuchung über die angelsächsischen Annalen bis zum Jahre 893*, Göttingen.

1889   M. Kupferschmidt, 'Über das Handschriftenverhältniss der Winchester-annalen', *Englische Studien* XIII, 165-87.

1900   H. H. Howorth, 'Notes on the Anglo-Saxon Chronicle', *English Historical Review* XV, 748-54.

1914   G. C. Donald, *Zur Entwicklung des Prosastils in der Sachsenchronik*, Marburg.

1917   M. L. R. Beaven, 'The regnal dates of Alfred, Edward the Elder and Athelstan', *English Historical Review* XXXII, 517-31.

1918   M. L. R. Beaven, 'The beginning of the year in the Alfredian chronicle', *English Historical Review* XXXIII, 328-42.

1922   J. R. Spaul, 'A note on The Anglo-Saxon Chronicle, ann. 897', *Notes and Queries* 12th S. X, 187-8.

1922   F. Viglione, *Studio Critico-Filologico su l'Anglo-Saxon Chronicle*, Pavia.

1924   R. H. Hodgkin, 'The beginning of the year in the English Chronicle', *English Historical Review* XXXIX, 497-510.

1925   F. M. Stenton, 'The south-western element in The Old English Chronicle' in *Essays in Medieval History presented to T. F. Tout*, Manchester, pp. 15-24, reprinted in *Preparatory to Anglo-Saxon England*, Oxford, pp. 106-115.

1933   A. J. Thorogood, 'The Anglo-Saxon Chronicle in the reign of Ecgberht', *English Historical Review* XLVIII, 353-63.

1935   F. P. Magoun, 'Territorial, place- and river-names in The Old English Chronicle A-text', *Harvard Studies and Notes on Philology and Literature* XVIII, 59-111.

1942   F. P. Magoun, 'King Alfred's naval and beach battle with the Danes in 896', *Modern Language Review* XXXVII, 409-14.

BIBLIOGRAPHY

1951   F. P. Magoun, 'King AEthelwulf's biblical ancestors', *Modern Language Review* XLVI, 249-50.

1954   R. Vaughan, 'The chronology of the Parker Chronicle 890-970', *English Historical Review* LXIX, 59-66.

1958   I. Lehiste, 'Names of Scandinavians in the Anglo-Saxon Chronicle', *Proceedings of the Modern Language Association of America* LXXIII, 6-22.

1971   C. Clark, 'The narrative mode of The Anglo-Saxon Chronicle before the Conquest' in *England before the Conquest*, ed. P. Clemoes and K. Hughes, Cambridge, pp. 215-35.

1971   R. H. C. Davis, 'Alfred the Great: propaganda and truth', *History* LVI, 169-82.

1974   R. Waterhouse, 'The Haesten episode in 894 Anglo-Saxon Chronicle', *Studia Neophilologica* XLVI, 136-41.

GLOSSARY

In the Glossary words will be found under the forms in which they occur, except that nouns and adjectives (excluding irregular comparatives, &c) will be found under the nom.sg. (masc.) and verbs under the infinitive (except that the present forms of ' to be ' will be found under *beon*, the pret. forms under *wæs*) ; pronouns under the nom.sg.masc. (except the 1st and 2nd pers. of the personal pronouns which will be found under the nom.sg. or the nom.pl. as the case may be). Irregular grammatical or phonological forms likely to offer difficulty are noted in their proper place with cross-references to the words under which they are dealt with. References where given are to annals or in the longer annals to annals and lines. When the reference is followed by * it indicates a restored or emended form and when followed by n it is a reference to the appropriate note. The order of le⁺ters is alphabetical, but *æ* is treated as a separate letter after *a* ; *þ*, *ð* after *t*. The OE characters *ƿ*, *ȝ*, *p* are replaced by *æ*, *g*, *w*. The prefix *ge-* is always ignored in the arrangement of the glossary. For abbreviations see *Deor* (ed. Kemp Malone) p. 32 or *Waldere* (ed. F. Norman), p. 49.

A

abbud, *m.a-stem, ABBOT* 890[1*]

ābisgian, *w.v.(2),* occupy, engage, 893[66]

ābrecan, *v.(5),* [ABREAK]; storm, attack, 860, 892[11]

ac, *conj.* [AC] ; but 893[58]

ācwelan, *v.(4),* [A + QUELE] ; die, perish, 893[83]

ādræfan, *w.v.(1b),* [ADREFE] ; drive away, banish 874, 878

ādrencan, *w.v.(1b),* [ADRENCH] ; drown (*trans.*) 890

ādrincan, *v.(3),* [ADRINK] ; to be drowned 853

āebbian, *w.v.(2),* [A + EBB] ; ebb away, recede ; **ahebbad,** *ppt.* 896[38]

āfaran, *v.(6),* [AFARE] ; go, depart, 894

āflieman, *w.v.(1b),* [AFLEME]͏ ; put to flight, expel, 836

āgan, *pret.-pres.(7),* [OWE] ; own. *sige ahton,* had the victory 833

āgān, *anom.v.,* [AGO] ; go away 896[31]

āgiefan, *v.(5),* [AGIVE] ; give up, restore ; **agef,** *p.t.* 893[58]

āhebbad, see **āebbian.**

āhōn, *v.(7),* [AHANG] ; to hang 896[49]

āhreddan, *w.v.(1a),* [AREDDE] ; rescue 893[34*]

ālædan, *w.v.(1b),* take away

ald, *adj.* OLD 885[31] ; the Elder (*byname*) 871[17]

56

aldorman, all, see **ealdormon, eall**

ān, *num.* ONE 878[18], 879[4], 885[16]; *indef.art.* A 874[7], 879[3]*; *adj.* alone 887[11]; *pron.* ONE 875[9], 896[32]

andlanᵹ, see **onlonᵹ**

ānlīpiᵹ, *adj.* [ONLEPY]; single, solitary, 871[40]n

ānstreces, *adv.* direct 893[92]n

ār, *f.ō-stem,* OAR 896[20]

āscūfan, *v.*(2), push off 896[46]

āsettan, *w.v.*(*1a*), [ASET]; (*with reflex.*) transport oneself 892[3]

āsittan, *v.*(5), [ASIT]; run aground

āþ, *m.a-stem,* OATH

āþīestrian, *w.v.*(2), [ATHESTER]; darken, be eclipsed 879

āweᵹ, *adv.* AWAY

āweorpan, *v.*(3), [AWARP]; cast out, overthrow, 867

āwerian, *w.v.*(*1a*), protect 885[4]

Æ

æfter, *prep.w.dat.,* AFTER 855 &c; along, through 878[6], 893[11]

æghwæþer (887), **æᵹþer** (893), *pron.* EITHER; each

æᵹþer, *conj.;* *æ. ge . . . ge,* both . . . and 893[69]

ælc, *pron.* EACH; *mæstra daga ælce,* almost every day 893[13]

ælc, *adj.* EACH, any, every 891

ælmesse, *f.n-stem,* ALMS 887[20]n

ænig, *adj.* ANY 893[10]

ær, *adv.* ERE, before, formerly 836, 876; previously 880; before this 885[17]; for the first time 851; first 896[45]; **ærest,** *superl.* first 890

ær, *conj.* ERE, before 877, &c; (*w.subj.*) 836

ær, *prep.w.dat.* before 885[15]

ærcebiscep (870), **erce-** (888), *m.a-stem,* ARCHBISHOP

æsc, *m.a-stem,* warship 896[19]

æt, *prep.w.dat.* AT 833; of 887[6]; on 896[24]

ætēowan, *w.v.*(*1b*), [ATEW]; appear, show, 891[16]

ætgædere, *adv.* together

B

bāt, *m.a-stem,* BOAT 891

be, bī (893[11]), *prep.w.dat.* BY 857; by, on 878[15], &c; on, to 871[38]; at 885[34]; along 893[25], 895[9]

bēaᵹ, *m.a-stem,* [BEE]; arm-ring, armlet, 876n

bearn, *n.a-stem,* [BAIRN]; child

beebbian, *w.v.*(2), strand (by the ebb tide) 896[40]

befæstan, *w.v.*(*1b*), secure, make safe 893[90]; entrust 886

bēgen, *adj.* [BO]; both 867 &c; **būtū** (*n.acc.*) 871[26]

begeondan, *prep.w.dat.* BEYOND

begietan, *v.*(5) [BEGET]; get; **begeton** (*p.t.pl.*) 896[3]

behindan, *adv.* BEHIND

behinon (878[17]), **behienan** (885[26]), *prep.w.dat.* on this side of

behorsian, *w.v.*(2), deprive of horses 885[6]

bēn, *f.i-stem,* [BENE]; request 885[34]

beniman, *v.*(4), [BENIM]; (*w. gen.*) deprive of 894[3]

bēon, *anom.v.* BE 891; **is,** *3sg.* is 878[27]; **sie,** *3sg.subj.* may be 891

berǣdan, *w.v.*(*1b*), deprive of 887[6*]

berōwan, *v.*(7), row past 896[48]

besittan, *v.*(5), [BESIT]; surround, besiege; **beseten,** *p.pt.* 893[44], 894[10]

bestelan, *v.(4),* [BESTEAL] ; (*w.reflex. and followed by gen.*) steal away from, 865, 876n, &c

betst, *adj.superl.* BEST 891

betweox (867), **betweoh** (890), **betwuh** (893[8]), *prep.w.dat.* between, amongst

bi, see **be**

biddan, *v.(5),* BID ; beg, pray 853

binnan, *adv.* [BIN] ; within 867

binnan, *prep.w.dat.* within 895[19]

biscep (845), **biscop,** (870), *m.a-stem,* BISHOP ; **biscepas,** *nom.pl.* 833

biscepsunu, *m.u-stem,* godson at confirmation, spiritual son, 853

bisceprīce, *n.ja-stem,* BISHOP-RIC, see, 867

bōcian, *w.v.(2),* [BOOK] ; grant by charter 855

bōclǣden, *n.a-stem,* [BOCLEDEN] (literary) Latin 891

geboren, *p.pt.* BORN 887[11]

brād, *adj.* BROAD 892[8]

brecan, *v.(4),* BREAK 885[37] ; attack, storm 851, 867

(ge)brengan, *w.v.(1b),* BRING 893[50], 895[10]

gebrocian, *w.v.(2),* destroy, crush 896[4] ; **gebrocede,** *p.pt.pl.* 896[5]

brōður, *m.r-stem,* BROTHER 860, &c ; (*g.sg.*) 887[5]

brycg, *f.jō-stem,* BRIDGE 887[1]

būan, *w.v.(3),* dwell ; **būgeað,** *3pl.pres.* 893[34] ; **būde,** *3sg.p.t.* 890

bufan, *prep.w.dat.* [BOVE] ; above

burg, *f.monos-stem,* BOROUGH ; city, fortified town ; strong-hold, fort 893[15], (*g.sg.*) 895[7]

burgware, *f.ō-stem* (*pl.*), towns-men, citizens 893[42]

būtan, -on, *prep.w.dat.* BUT ; without 891, 893[15] ; except (for), apart from, 878, 886[4]n ; outside 893[97]

būtan, -on, *adv.* without, out-side 867, 893[96]

būte, *conj.* BUT 896[22]

būton, *conj.* except that 889

būtū, see **bēgen**

C

cēap, *m.a-stem,* [CHEAP] ; prop-erty, possessions, (*g.sg.*) 893[96]

ceaster, *f.ō-stem,* fort, city, 867 &c.

cēosan, *v.(2),* CHOOSE 890* , elect 870.

cirice, *f.n-stem,* CHURCH 874

cirlisc, *adj.* CHURLISH ; com-mon, rustic, 892[12]

cirr, *m.i-stem,* time, occasion 896[24]

gecirran, *w.v.(1b),* [I-CHERRE] ; submit 878, 886 ; *to þam gecirdon,* resolved this 867 ; *to anum gecierdon,* united 835

cniht, *m.a-stem,* KNIGHT ; boy 893[58]

corn, *n.a-stem,* CORN 893[96]

crismlīsing, *f.ō-stem,* baptism 878[39]n

Cristna, *m.n-stem,* CHRISTIAN ; Englishman 893[85]

cuēn, *f.i-stem,* QUEEN 888 ; *hæfde to cuene,* had married 836, &c

cuman, *v.(4),* COME ; *c. ute,* were outside 893[18] ; *c. onweg,* escape 896[34] ; **cuōm,** *p.t.sg.* 835 &c ; **cōm** 855, 878[25] ; **cuōmon,** *p.t.pl.* 891, **cōmon** 885[9] ; **cōme,** *p.t.subj.* 893[58]

cumpæder, *m.a-stem,* fellow godfather, gossip, 893[60] (Lat. *compater*)

58

cweþan, *v.*(5), [QUETHE] ; say
cwild, *m.* or *f.i-stem*, death,
mortality ; *ceapes* c.7 *monna*,
murrain and plague, 896⁶
cynerīce, *n.ja-stem*, [KINNRICK] ;
kingdom, realm 871³⁸
cyning, *m.a-stem*, KING 833 ;
kyning 878³⁴ ; cyng 860,
893³⁸ ; cinges (*g.sg.*) 893⁷³
cynn, *n.ja-stem*, KIN ; race
893⁷⁶

D

dæg, *m.a-stem*, DAY, time, 851,
871³⁶
dæges, *adv.* by day 893⁹²
dǣl, *m.i-stem*, DEAL ; share,
part,
gedǣlan, *w.v.*(1b), DEAL, share
out, 876
Denisc, *adj.* DANISH ; the Danish pattern 896³³ ; *ða Deniscan*, the Danes 896³⁶
dēop, *n.a-stem*, the DEEP, channel, 896³⁶
dohtor, *f.r-stem*, DAUGHTER
dōn, *anom.v.* DO 853, 895¹¹
gedōn, *anom.v.* [I-DO] ; do
896²⁵ ; arrive 893⁷¹
drǣfan, *w.v.*(1b), [D R E F E] ;
drive 887¹⁸
dreccan, *w.v.*(1b), [DRETCH] ;
oppress, harass 896¹⁵
drȳge, *adj.* DRY ; *on drygum*, on
dry land 896³⁰

E

ēa, *f.ō-stem*, [EA] ; river, (*acc.*)
895¹⁰ ; ēas, *g.sg.* 895¹³, ē,
g.sg. 893⁸⁰⁴ ; ēi, *d.sg.* 875 ;
ēæ 895⁹
ēac, *prep.w.dat.* also, in addition
to, 878²³, &c
ēaca, *m.n-stem*, [EKE] ; increase,
reinforcement 893⁶⁹

ealdormon (893⁵⁵), -man
(893⁷³), aldormon (837),
-man (845), *m.monos-stem*,
ALDERMAN, chief officer of a
scir, 837n
eal(l), *n.a-stem*, ALL, everything, 893⁴⁹, (*w.gen.*) 893⁹⁶ ;
mid ealle, and everything
892⁴, &c
eall, *adj., pron.* ALL, 890, 893⁸ ;
al, *acc.n.sg.* 855 ; all 870 ;
alle, *acc.f.sg.* 865 ; alne,
acc.m.sg. 853 ; alle, *acc.pl.*
853 ; allum, *d.sg.* 860 ; *d.pl.*
in *on allum þam*, with all
those 874¹⁰
eall, *adv.* altogether 893⁹⁶ ;
in its (their) entirety 893¹⁸
ealles, *adv.* altogether 896⁴
earc, *f.ō-stem*, ARK 855²⁷
ēas, see ēa
ēast, *adv.* in the EAST 886 ;
eastward 891
ēastan, *adv.* from the east ; *be
eastan*, on the east of 893⁷⁵
ēast-ende, *m.ja-stem*, EAST-END
892⁶
ēasteweard, *adj.* eastern 865
ēasteweardes, *adv.* to the
east 893⁴⁰
ēastlang, *adv.* eastwards, extending east, 892⁷
ēast-rīce, *n.ja-stem*, the eastern
kingdom, Austrasia, 892²,
893²
ēastron, *f.n-stem* (*pl.*), EASTER
ēce, *adj.*, ECHE ; eternal 855
efenēhð(o), *f.ō-stem*, neighbourhood 893⁹⁹n
efes, *f.ō-stem*, EAVES ; edge, side,
893¹²
efor, *m.a-stem*, [EVER] ; wild
boar 885¹⁶
eft, *adv.* [EFT.] ; again
ēi, see ēa
ende, *m.ja-stem*, END 893⁴⁶n

elþīodignes, *f.jō-stem,* pilgrimage 891

Englisc, *adj.* ENGLISH 896 ; the English language 891

eorl, *m.a-stem,* jarl 871[2]n

ercebiscop, see **ærcebiscep**

ergan, *w.v.(1a),* [EAR] ; plough 876

F

faran, *v.(6),* FARE, go 851 ; *(p.t.subj.pl.)* would go 876 ; *(reflex.)* went 855 ; *of f.* abandon 893[20]

gefaran, *v.(6),* [IFARE] ; go, depart, 877 ; die 855, 867, &c

fæder, *m.r-stem,* FATHER

fædren-healf, *f.ō-stem),* paternal side 887[10]

gefægen, *adj.* FAIN ; glad *(w.gen.)* 855, 878[18]

fær, *n.a-stem,* FARE ; journey ; *on fære* on his way 893[29]

færeld, *n.a-stem,* journey, pilgrimage 889

fæsten, *n.ja-stem,* stronghold, fortification 877, 885[3]

fēa, *adj.* FEW ; a few 892[11]

feaxed, *ppt.,* [FAXED] ; long-haired, 891[17]

fela, *n.indecl. (orig.u-stem) w.gen.* [FELE] ; many 871[19], &c

feld, *m.u-stem,* FIELD ; open country 893[10]n

fenn, *m. or n.ja-stem,* FEN 892[12]n.

feoh, *n.a-stem (orig.u-stem),* FEE ; goods, property, 865, 878[31], &c

feoh-gehāt, *n.a-stem,* promise of money 865

feohlēas, *adj.* moneyless 896[2]

gefeoht, *n.a-stem,* FIGHT, battle, fighting, 868, &c

(ge)feohtan, *v.(3),* FIGHT 833, &c

feor, *adv.* FAR 882

feorh, *m.u-stem,* life 855[18]

fēorða, *adj.* FOURTH 851

fēower, *adj.* FOUR 882

fēowertig, *num.(w.gen.),* FORTY 893[36]

gefēra, *m.n-stem,* [YFERE] ; companion, servant 878[30]

fēran, *w.v.(1b),* [FERE] ; go, proceed, 835, &c

ferian, *w.v.(1a),* FERRY ; carry, transport 893[21], 893[33]

gefetian, *w.v.(2),* [YFET] ; fetch, take away ; **gefetedon** 895[17]

fierd (867), **fird** (894[7]), *f.i-stem,* [FERD] ; levy, army, esp. West Saxon army, 835, &c ; *d.sg.* from the army 876

fierdian, *w.v.(2),* serve, be on military service, 893[30]

fierdlēas, *adj.* without army, unguarded, 893[12]

fīf, *num.* FIVE 896[33]

flēam, *m.a-stem,* [FLEME] ; flight 893[87]

flēon, *v.(2),* FLEE 893[25]

geflīeman, *w.v.(1b),* [FLEME] ; put to flight, drive away, 835, &c ; *(p.pt.pl.)* 871[19]

flocc, *m.a-stem,* FLOCK ; troop 893[13]

flocrād, *f.ō-stem,* gang, troop 893[12]

flōd, *f. ō-stem,* FLOOD ; tide 896[45]

folc, *n.a-stem,* FOLK 878 ; body of men 893[40]

folc-gefeoht, *n.a-stem,* battle 871[37], 887[16]

fōn, *v.(7),* [FANG] ; seize, receive, get ; *feng to rice,* succeeded to (took) the throne 836, &c

gefōn, *v.(7),* [IFANG] ; take, seize 851, 893[21]

for, *prep.* FOR, through, 891 ; 893[9]n

foran, *adv.* [FORNE] ; from in front 893[23]

forbærnan, *w.v.(1b)*, [FORBURN] ; burn up 893[51]

foregīsl, *m.a-stem,* (preliminary) hostage 877, &c

foresprecen, *p.pt.* [FORESPOK-EN] ; 885[1], 895[1]

forfaran, *v.(6)*, obstruct 896[27]

forhergian, *w.v.(2)*, ravage 887[17]

forlǣtan, *v.(7)*, [FORLET] ; leave, abandon, 885[6], 895[14]

forrīdan, *v.(1)*, ride before ; intercept, cut off, 893[13], 893[97]

forslægen, *p.pt.* slain 882

forswīðe, *adv.* utterly 896[4]

forþ, *adv.* FORTH, forward, on, 887[18], 893[41]

forþǣm, *conj.* because 887[10], &c

forþfēran, *w.v.(1b)*, depart, die

forþon þe, *conj.* because 891

forðȳ ðe, *conj.* [FORTHY] ; because 894[3], 896[34]

forweorþan, *v.(3)*, [FORWORTH] ; perish, be lost, 877, &c

forwiernan, *w.v.(1b)*, FORWARN ; withhold, deny, 895[8]

forwundian, *w.v.(2)*, [FOR-WOUND] ; wound 882, 896[51]

forwyrcan, *w.v.(1b)*, [FOR-WORK] ; obstruct, barricade, 895[10]

fram (892[11]), **from** (872), *prep.* *w.dat.* FROM ; by 838

gefrēogan, *w.v.(2)*, *orig.(3)*, [YFREE] ; befriend, honour 885[33]

Frēsisc, *adj.* Frisian 896[43] ; the Frisian pattern 896[22]

fretan, *v.(5)*, [FRET] ; eat, eat to the bone 893[82]

frettan, *w.v.(1b)*, eat, eat bare 893[98]

friþ, *m.a-stem* (*orig.u-stem*), [FRITH] ; peace, *friþ nam* made peace 876, &c

from, see **fram**

fulluht-nama, *m.n-stem,* baptismal name 890

fulnēah, *adv.* FULL NIGH, almost 896[19]

fultum, *m.a-stem,* [FULTUM] ; help 893[42]

(ge)fultumian, *w.v.(2)*, help, support, 836, &c ; (*p.t.subj.*) 853

fulwiht, *n.a-stem* (*orig.f.i-stem*), [FULLOUGHT] ; baptism 878[14]

furlang, *n.a-stem,* FURLONG 896[38]

furþum, *adv.* [FORTHEN] ; already, just, 895[12]

gefylce, *n.ja-stem,* troop, division, 871[12] ; *d.pl.* 871[15]

gefyrn, *adv.* [FERN] ; before, formerly, 892[2]

G

gegadrian, *w.v.(2)*, GATHER 867

gān, *anom.v.* GO 885[5], &c. See **hond**

gegān, *anom.v.* [IGO] ; subdue, overrun, 870, 874

gangdagas, *m.a-stem* (*pl.*) [GANGDAYS] ; Rogation Days 891

ge, *conj.* [YE] ; *ge . . . ge . . .* both . . . and . . . 835, &c

gēar, *n.a-stem,* YEAR 836, &c ; **gere** (*d.sg.*) 894[1] ; **ger** (*acc. pl.*) 894[16]

gearo, *adj.* [YARE] ; ready for, prepared for, 874

giefan, *v.(5)*, GIVE ; give in marriage 853, 855

gif, *conj.* IF 893[10]

gifu, *f.ō-stem,* [GIVE] ; gift 885[24]

gioncg, *adj.* YOUNG, (*as byname*) 871[18]

gīsl, *m.a-stem,* [YISEL] ; hostage 874

God, *m.a-stem,* GOD 855
gŏd, *adj.* GOOD 860 ; considerable 837
godsunu, *m.u-stem,* GODSON 890

H

habban, *w.v.(3),* HAVE *(auxil.)* 836, &c ; possess, hold 867 ; marry 885³⁰
haldan, see **healdan**
hālga, *m.n-stem,* saint ; *ealra haligra mæssa,* All Hallows' Day 900 ; **halechen** *(d.pl.)* 890
(ge)hālgian, *w.v.(2),* HALLOW, consecrate 853, 887⁸
hālig, *adj.* HOLY 876
hām, *m.a-stem,* HOME 893¹⁶
hāmweard, *adv.* HOMEWARD, home, 855, &c.
hāmweardes, *adv.* HOMEWARDS ; on its way home 893³¹
(ge)hātan, *v.(7),* [HIGHT] ; name, call, 891, &c ; promise 865¹ ; bid, command, 896
gehāwian, *w.v.(2),* observe, notice, 895⁹
hæftnīede, *f.i-stem,* domination, custody, 886
hǣlo, *f.in-stem,* [HEAL] ; salvation 855 *(d.sg.)*
hærfest, *m.a-stem,* HARVEST, autumn, 877, 895⁶
hǣt, from **hātan**
hǣþen, *adj.* HEATHEN ; *hǣþne men,* the Scandinavians 832, &c
hē, *pron.m.* HE 835 ; **hine** (836), **hiene** (853), *acc.* him 853, it 878²⁰, 891 *(reflex.)* 865, &c ; **his,** *gen.* of him 878¹⁷, his 836, &c ; **him,** *dat.* him 838, &c, it 878²⁰, to him, his 885²¹, 893³⁴, *(reflex.)* 855,

&c ; **hire,** *f.gen.* her 888, **hiere,** of it 878¹⁷n ; **hit,** *n,* it 860, 877 (cf **sum**)
healdan (860), **haldan** (874, 886), *v.(7),* HOLD, keep, rule.
healf, *f.ō-stem,* HALF ; side 887¹⁵
healf, *adj.* HALF, *(n.pl.)* 893¹⁶ ; *oþrum (þridde, feorðe) healfum* one (two, three) and a half 851, 900, &c
hefelīc, *adj.* [HEAVILY] ; heavy, serious, hard, 868
hēr, *adv.* HERE ; at this place in the annals 832, &c
here, *m.ja-stem,* [HERE] ; band of robbers ; the Danish army 837⁵n ; **herige** (838), **here** (875), *d.sg.* ; **heres** 878¹⁰n.
herehÿþ, *f.i-stem,* booty, plunder, 885, 893³¹
hergian, *w.v.(2),* HARROW ; plunder, seize, 875, &c
hergaþ, *m.a-stem (orig.u-stem,* harrying, plundering raid, 893⁴⁷
hider, *adv.* HITHER 893¹⁰⁰
hīe, *pron.pl.* they 835, 882 ; **hī** 887⁹ ; **hīe,** *acc.* them 871³, 896³⁹ ; **hī** 891 ; *(reflex.)* 876⁵, 891 ; **hiora** 892¹⁰, **heora** 893⁶, **hiera** 867, **hira** 896⁴⁰, *gen.* of them 875, &c, their 867, theirs 896⁴⁶, *(obj.)* them 893⁵⁵ ; *(reflex.)* for themselves 876n ; **him,** *dat.* (for) them 835, 896²⁸ ; *(reflex.)* for themselves 896³
hīera, *adj.comp.* HIGHER 896²¹
hīeran, *w.v.(1b),* HEAR 851, &c
gehīersum, *adj.* [HEARSUM] ; submissive, obedient 853
hīersumian, *w.v.(2),* [HEARSUM] ; make obedient, subject, *(p.t.subj.)* 853
hindan, *adv.* in the rear, from behind, 877, 893⁷⁸

hléapere, *m.ja-stem*, courier, messenger, 889

hlōþ, *f.ō-stem*, band (of robbers) 879, 893[11]n

hond, *f.u-stem*, HAND ; side 853, 871[8] ; *to his honda*, at his hand, of him 887[9] ; *on hond eodon* submitted, surrendered to 882

hors, *n.a-stem*, HORSE 892[4]

hors-þegn, *m.a-stem*, horse-thane, marshal 896[12], 896[53]

gehorsud, -od, *p.pt*. [YHORSED]; supplied with horses, mounted, 866, &c

hrædlíce, *adv*. [RADLY] ; quickly 876

hund, *num*. [HUND] ; hundred 851, (892[5])

hundtwelftig, *num*. (*n.a-stem*), hundred and twenty 892[7]

hungor, *m.a-stem* (*orig.u-stem*), HUNGER 893[83]

hwǣr, *conj*. WHERE 895[9]

hwǣr, *adv*. WHERE 891

gehwæþer, hwaþer, *adj*. WHETHER ; which 893[12] ; either, each, 853, 871[7]

hwelc, *adj*. WHICH ; *swa hwelc* whatsoever 874

hwíl, *f.ō-stem*, WHILE, time, 837 ; *þa hwile þe . . . lengest* as long as 893[27]

hwílum, *adv*. WHILOM, at times, sometimes, 891

hȳd, *f.i-stem*, HIDE, skin, 891

I

ic, *pron*. I 893[64]

íggaŏ, *m.a-stem*, [AIT] ; island 893[36]

ígland, *n.a-stem*, ISLAND 894[9]

ilca, *adj*. [ILK] ; same

in, *adv*. IN 893[22]

in, *prep.w.dat*. IN, amongst, 878[26], 893[34]

innan, *prep.w.acc*. [INNE] ; in, into, 868, &c

inne, *adv*. [INNE] ; within, inside, 867, &c

intō, *prep.w.dat*. INTO 876, &c

L

lāf, *f.ō-stem*, [LAVE] ; remainder 867, &c

lang, *adj*. LONG 891 ; **lengra**, *comp*. 892[8] ; **lengest**, *superl. adv*. 893[27] (see **hwíl**)

langscip, *n.a-stem*, warship 896[19]

lārēow, *m.wa-stem*, [LAREW] ; teacher 891

late, *adv*. LATE 867

(ge)lǣdan, *w.v.(1b)*, LEAD, take, convey, 871[8], &c

lǣs, *adv*. LESS 900

lǣstan, *w.v.(1b)*, [LAST] ; follow, serve, 874

gelǣstan, *w.v.(1b)*, [YLAST] ; do, perform, 878[24]

gelend, *p.pt*. landed, arrived 886 ; gone 893[61]

lengra, lengest, see **lang**

lēod, *f.ō-stem*, [LEDE] ; (*in pl.*) people 855

lēoma, *m.n-stem*, [LEAM] ; beam of light 891

líc, *n.a-stem*, [LICH] ; body, corpse, 855, 860, &c

licgan, *v.(5)*, LIE, rest ; **líþ**, *3sg.pres*. 855, &c ; *liŏ ut*, flows out 892[9]

lof, *n.a-stem*, [LOF] ; praise, glory, 855

gelōme, *adv*. [YLOME] ; frequently 887[16]

lond, *n.a-stem*, LAND 855, &c ; district 870

longe, *adv*. LONG, for a long time 871[16]

lufu, *f.ō-stem*, LOVE 891[7]n

lȳtel, *adj.* LITTLE, small, (*instr. sg.*) 871[35], 878[6]n

M

mā, *sb.indecl.* more 896[20]

manig, see **monig**

mæsse, *f.n-stem*, MASS, feast, 900

mǣst, *adj.superl.* MOST 893[13]; greatest 851; greater 878

meahte (877), **mehte**, *pret.- pres.*(5), could 893[10]; (*subj.*) MIGHT 896[45]; *mehte to, to mehte*, could get to, could reach, 877, 896[37]

mētan, *w.v.*(*1b*), MEET, come up, 868, 877, &c

gemētan, *w.v.*(*1b*), meet, oppose, 871[3]

mete, *m.i-stem*, MEAT; food, provisions, 891, 893[27]

metelīest, *f.i-stem*, lack of food, famine, 893[82]

micel, *sb.w.gen.* much, a great part, 878

micel, *adj.* [MICKLE]; big, great

micle, *adv.* much 896[5]

miclum, *adv.* greatly 878[30], 882

mid, *prep.w.dat.* [MID]; with, along with 851, &c; accompanied by 835, &c. See **sē**

mid, *adv.* with them, present, 885[25], 893[6]

mid(d), *adj.* MID 878, &c

middelrīce, *n.ja-stem*, middle kingdom 887[13]

mīl, *f.jō-stem*, MILE 892[8]

mon, *m.monos-stem*, MAN 832, 878[10]n

mon, *indef.pron.* ONE 871[41], &c

mōnaþ, *m.þ-stem*, MONTH, 836, &c

monig (838), **manig** (896[14]), *pron.* MANY

monig, *adj.* MANY, many a, 853, &c

mōrfæsten, *n.ja-stem*, moorstronghold 878

munt, *m.a-stem*, mountain, (*pl.*) Alps 887[15]

mūþa, *m.n-stem*, mouth (of a river), estuary, 845, &c

N

nā, *adv.* NO; not, never, 893[94]; *na ne*, not at all, never 871[41]

nān, *pron.* NONE 887[10], 896[37]

nān, *adj.* NO 868, &c

nāwðer, *conj.* [NAUTHER]; *nawðer ne . . . ne*, neither . . . nor 896[22]

næfde, *3sg.p.t.* had not 896[3]

næs, *3sg.p.t.* was not 887[10], &c; **nǣron**, *pl.* were not 896[22]

ne, *adv.* not 871[41], &c

nēah, *adv.* NIGH, near 894[11]; **nīehst**, *superl.* nearest 878[13], 893[8]n

genēat, *m.a-stem*, [GENEAT]; follower, dependant, 896[43]n

nēawest, *f.i-stem*, neighbourhood 895[6]

nemnan, *w.v.*(*1b*), [NEMN]; call, name, mention, 891, &c

nerian, *w.v.*[*1a*), save, rescue 893[88]

nīehst, see **nēah**

nigon, *num.* NINE 896[27]

nigontēoþa, *adj.* NINETEENTH 855 (cf **healf**)

niht, *f.monos-stem*, NIGHT, nighttime, 865, &c

nihtes, *adv.* by night 876, &c

niman, *v.*(*4*), [NIM]; take 876, &c; adopt 853; *sige nom*, won the victory 837, &c

geniman, *v.*(*4*), take, seize, capture, 882

nīwe, *adj.* NEW 896[37]

nōlǣs, *adv.(as sb.)*, no less
896[51]

noldon, *3pl.* would not do 876

nōm, see **niman**

norþ, *adv.* NORTH 893[36]

norþan, *adv.* from the North ; *be
norþan* on the north of 893[75]

norþerne, *adj.* NORTHERN 890

norþsǣ, *f.i-stem*, the Bristol
Channel 893[37]n

norþweardes, *adv.* NORTH-
WARDS 893[21]

ġenotud, *p.pt.* used up 893[29]n

nytwyrðe, *adj.* useful 896[23]

O

of, *prep.w.dat.* OF, by 890 ; out
of, from 836, &c ; *þær . . .
of* therefrom 891

of, *adv.* OFF, away, 896[30]

ofer, *prep.w.acc.* OVER, through,
851, &c ; throughout 855 ;
across 867, &c ; beyond,
after, 853, 878 ; contrary to
893[4] ; after 871[30]

ofer, *adv.* across 892[4]

oferherġan, *w.v.(2)*, overrun
865 ; **oferherġeadon** 832

offaran, *v.(6)*, pursue, overtake.
893[77], 893[94]

ofrīdan, *v.(1)*, overtake 877

ofslēan, *v.(6)*, [OFSLAY] ; slay
837, 871[20]

oft, *adv.* OFT, often, 875* ;
oftor, *comp.* more often 893[18]

on, *adv.* ON ; therein 892[12]

on, *prep.w.acc.* ON 871[41], &c ;
into 836, &c ; against 835 ;
in accordance with 896[22] ;
w.dat. on 887[10] ; in, amongst,
838, &c ; inside 868 ; in,
during 860[4], 865, &c

ond (894[1]), *conj.* AND 853, &c ;
but 837, 871[36], &c ; usually
by the ampersand 7

onlong (882), **andlang** (887[2])
prep.w.gen. ALONG

ondweard, *adj.* present 851*

onforan, *prep.w.acc.* [AFORE] ;
before, at the beginning,
893[90]

onfōn, *v.(7)*, [ONFANG] ; receive
878[28], 893[55] (*w.gen.*)

onġēan, *prep.w.acc.* against, to,
to meet, 893[22] ; **onġēn** 878[16],
896[19]

onġietan, *v.(5)*, [ANGET] ; per-
ceive ; **onġet** 895[13]

onġinnan, *v.(3)*, [ONGIN] ; begin 895[12]

onwald, *m.a-stem*, [ONWALD] ;
rule, dominion, 900

onweġ, *adv.* AWAY 896[34*]

oþ, *prep.w.acc.* until, up to, 851 ;
to, as far as, up to, 868, &c

ōþer, *pron.* OTHER ; the other(s)
875, &c ; the rest 851, 893[83] ;
oþer . . . oþer, (the) one . . .
the other 871[12], 893[54]

ōþer, *adj.* OTHER 892[16] ; another,
second, 885[3], 893[61] ; *oþer . . .
oþer*, one . . . the other 88[2],
893[19]

oðrōwan, *v.(7)*, row away 896[44]

oþþæt, *conj.* until 885[4], &c

oþþe, *conj.* until 893[41] ; or
891 ; *oþþe . . . oþþe*, either
. . . or 893[51]

oðwindan, *v.(3)*, escape 896[32]

P

pāpa, *m.n-stem*, POPE 885[23]

R

rād, *f.ō-stem*, [ROAD] ; raid
871[41]

ġerǣcan, *w.v.(1b)*, REACH, deal
with, 893[10] ; overtake 894[7] ;
capture 885[11]

ræde, *adj.* mounted 891

rædlīce, *adv.* [REDLY]; skilfully 887[17]

reccan, *w.v.*(*1b*), RECK, care, (*p.t.pl.*) 891

gerēfa, *m.n-stem*, REEVE 896[42*]n

gerēþru, *n.*(*pl.*) steering gear 891

rīce, *n.ja-stem*, [RICHE]; kingdom, dominion, authority, throne, 836, &c

rīcsian, *w.v.*(2), rule 836, &c

rīdan, *v.*(*1*), RIDE 870, &c

gerīdan, *v.*(*1*), *tr.* override, occupy, 878[2], 878[4]; *intr.* ride 878[14]

rīman, *w.v.*(*1b*), [RIME]; count 871

rīp, *n.*(*a-stem*), [RIPE]; crop, harvest, 895[8]

rōd, *f.ō-stem*, ROOD, cross, 885[86]

rōhton, see reccan

rȳmet, *n.ja-stem*, room, space, 893[8]

gerȳpan, *v.*(*1*), [RIPE]; reap 895[7]

S

salde, see sellan

same, *adv.* likewise 891[17]n

samnian, *w.v.*(2), [SAM]; gather, muster, 893[19]

samworht, *p.pt.* half-constructed 892[18]

sārgian, *w.v.*(2), WOUND 896[47]

sǣ, *f.i-stem*, SEA 874, &c

sǣ-rima, *m.n-stem*, [SEARIM]; sea-shore 896[26]

gescæpen, *p.pt.* shaped, built, 896[22]

sceoldon, *3pl.þ.t.* SHOULD 887[10]; scolden (*subj.*) were to 893[17]

scip, *n.a-stem*, SHIP 851; scipo, *acc.pl.* 885[11]

sciphere, *m.ja-stem*, fleet, esp. the Danish fleet 835, &c; the English fleet 875

sciphlæst, *m.a-stem*, ship-load, crew, 833, &c

scipian, *w.v.*(2), SHIP, embark 892[3]

scīr, *f.ō-stem*, SHIRE; division (of the army) 893[30]

scōl, *f.ō-stem*, SCHOOL, hostel, 874n, 885[24]

scolden, see sceoldon

sē, *dem.pron.* that, it; þā, *acc. f.sg.* it 893[21]; þæt, *n.nom.* that, it 887[8], &c, *acc.* 835; 7 þæt, which 878[27]; þæs, *g.sg.* of it, of him, 855; þǣm, *n.dat.sg.* that, it, 894[1], 896[33], þām 855; tō þǣm, to such an extent 896[47]; mid þǣm þæt, in that (*conj.*) 896[6]; þā, *n.pl.* these 896[33], those. the latter 882, 893[37], 893[40]; *acc.pl.* them 885[10]; þām *d.pl.* 871[39], 874. Often indistinguishable (as 885[17], &c) from

sē, *rel.pron.m.* who 885[29], which 878[18]; þæs, *g.sg.* whose 890; sīo, *f.n.sg.* who 888, sēo which 893[93]; þæt, *neut.n.sg.* which 886, 890, &c

sē, *dem.adj.m.* this, that, 836, &c; þæs, *neut.g.sg.* þæs geares that year 871[37], þæs ilcan wintra, in that same winter 878[7]; þā, *f.acc.sg.* 887[14]; þā, *n.pl.* those 882, often indistinguishable from

sē, *def.art.m.* the 833, &c; þone, *acc.sg.* 837; þæs, *g.sg.* 871[39]; þām, *d.sg.* 838, þǣm 892[9]; sēo, *f.nom.sg.* 892[9], sīo 879; ðā, *f.acc.sg.* 885[3]; þǣre, *f.g.sg.* 885[36]; þǣre, *f.d.sg.* 867, 885[12]; þæt, *neut. sg.* 896[32]; *acc.* 851, &c; þæs, *neut.g.sg.* 894[3]; þām, *neut.d.sg.* 868; þȳ, *neut.instr.*

sg. 871³⁸ ; **þā**, *n.pl.* 881 ;
þāra, *g.pl.* 893⁸² ; **þǣm**,
d.pl. 893⁴¹

sēcan, *w.v.(1b)*, SEEK, make for,
867, 893¹⁰

secgan, *w.v.(3)*, SAY, tell, 851 ;
sǣde *1sg.pret.* 893⁴⁴

self, *adj.* SELF 855, &c

sellan, *w.v.(1b)*, SELL ; give,
grant, 893⁵⁶ ; **salde** 836, 874 ;
saldon 877, **sealdon** 874

sendan, *w.v.(1b)*, SEND 853

seofon, *num.adj.* SEVEN 891

seofoða, *adj.* SEVENTH 878¹⁴

set, *n.a-stem*, habitation, camp,
893¹⁸

gesettan, *w.v.(1a)*, SET ; build,
restore, 886

sex (896¹⁵), **syx** (900) *num.adj.*
SIX

sibsumnes, *f.jō-stem*, [SIB-
SOMENESS] ; peace 860

simle, *adv.* always, constantly,
893¹⁶

sīo, see **sē**

sige, *m.i-stem*, [SIƷE] ; victory

sigelan, *w.v.(1b)*, SAIL 877

sittan, *v.(5)*, SIT, remain, stay,
851, &c

gesittan, *v.(5)*, settle, remain,
874, 879 ; *(p.pt.)* stayed,
finished, 893²⁸n

sīþ, *m.a-stem*, [SITHE] ; journey
892⁴ ; time, occasion, 893¹⁹

siþþan, *adv.* [SITHEN] ; after-
wards 893¹¹

slēan, *v.(6)*, SLAY ; *micel wæl
geslog*, &c, made great slaughter 837, &c

sōna, *adv.* SOON 885⁷

standan, *v.(6)*, STAND, be, 891,
896¹⁹

stǣlhere, *m.ja-stem*, predatory
band 896¹⁷

stǣlwyrð, *adj.* [STALWORTH] ;
serviceable 895¹⁸

stæþ, *n.a-stem*, STAITH ; (river-)
bank 893⁷⁸ ; shore, sea-shore,
896¹⁶

stede, *m.i-stem*, STEAD, place 887

stemn, *m.(a-stem)*, period of service 893²⁸

steorra, *m.n-stem*, STAR 891

sum, *adj.* SOME, a, 893³⁵, &c ;
one 895⁸ ; *hie sume*, some of
them 867, *hit sum*, some of it
877, *sumum þam here*, part of
the army 875

sum, *pron.* one 878²⁶n ; some
877

sumor, *m.u-stem*, SUMMER 875

sumorlida, *m.n-stem*, summer
army 871³⁰n

sunne, *f.n-stem*, SUN 879

sunu, *m.u-stem*, SON 851

sūþ, *adv.* SOUTH 851

sūþan, *adv.* from the south ; *be
suþan* to the south of 871³⁸

sūð-rima, *m.n-stem*, south
coast 896⁵²

sūð-stæð, *n.a-stem*, south coast
896¹⁶

swā, *adv.* SO, in such a way,
853, 878²⁵, &c ; *swa hwaþerre
swa*, whichever 893¹⁸ ; *eac
swa*, likewise, moreover, 895² ;
7 eac swa, and so he did also
893⁵⁷

swā, *conj.* as, even as, 885²⁷ ;
swa . . . swa, so (as) . . .
as 874, &c ; *swa swa*, so that
894⁷ ; *sona swa*, as soon as
885⁹

sweostor, *f.r-stem*, sister 888

swerian, *v.(6)*, SWEAR 874

swift, adj. SWIFT 896²¹

swiðe, *adv.* [SWITH] ; greatly
896¹⁶ ; very 893⁴⁰ ; **swiþor**,
comp. more, more severely,
896⁵ ; *superl.* in *ealles swiþost,
ealra swiþust*, most of all
896⁸, 896¹⁷

T

tēon, *v.(2)*, [TEE] ; draw, tow, 892¹⁰, 894¹⁵

tēoþa, *adj. TENTH* 855

tīd, *f.i-stem*, TIDE ; hour 879

tilian, *w.v.(2)*, TILL ; gain a livelihood 876n

timbran, *w.v.(1b)*, build 898¹⁸

tō, *prep.w.acc.* TO 836 ; *w.gerund* 886 ; *w.dat.* to 885 ; to, for, 855, 874 ; as 836, 885²¹ ; see **hond**

tō, *adv.* TO ; thereto 887⁸ ; up 893⁴⁸ ; forth 896²⁷

tōbrecan, *v.(5)*, [TOBREAK] ; break up, break in pieces, 893⁵¹, &c

tōcuman, *v.(4)*, come, arrive, 893⁴⁵

tōdǣlan, *w.v.(1b)*, separate, divide, 885¹, 887⁷

tōfaran, *v.(6)*, disperse, scatter, 896¹

tōniman, *v.(4)*, divide, split, 893¹⁶

trēow, *f.wō-stem*, pledge, treaty, 893⁵

getruma, *m.n-stem*, troop 871¹⁵

tū, *adv.* twice 896¹⁹

tū, see **twēgen**

tugon, see **tēon**

tūn, *m.a-stem*, TOWN ; enclosure 867n

tuwwa, *adv.* twice 893¹⁸

twēgen, **tuēgen**, *num.(adj.)m.* TWAIN, two, 833, &c ; **twā**, *neut.* 885²³, **tū** 882, 887³ ; **twǣm**, *dat.* 871¹², **twām** 887⁴

twelf, *num.adj.* TWELVE 893¹

tuelfta, *adj.* TWELFTH 878

þ

þā, *adv.* [THO] ; then 835³, 851¹ᶜ

þā, *conj.* þa . . . þa when 885¹¹, 893³⁰

þā, see **sē**

geþafung, *f.ō-stem*, consent, acquiescence 887⁸

þāra, *adv.* there 887³

þara, see **sē**

þǣr, *adv.* THERE 833, &c

þǣr, *conj.* where, 877, 893⁸

þǣron, *adv.* THEREON 882

þǣrtō, *adv.* thereby 895¹³

þæs, *adv.* after 871³⁰, *þæs on Eastron* the Easter after 878¹⁰, *þæs ymb iii niht* three nights after 871²

þæs þe, *conj.* from the time when, after 855⁹, 874

þæs, see **sē**

þæt, *conj.* THAT, so that 853

þæt, see **sē**

þe, *rel.pron.* who, that, which, 851, 871³⁹ ; whom 885³⁰ ; that, in which, when, 885¹⁹, &c ; where 896³⁶ ; *þe . . . his*, whose 885³⁰

þe, *conj.* than 900

þe, *part.* see **forþon**, **þæs**, &c

þēah, *adv.* however, nevertheless 867, &c ; **þēh** 896⁴⁵

þearf, *f.ō-stem*, [THARF] ; profit, advantage, 874

þegn, *m.a-stem*, THANE 871⁴⁰n ; **þēna** (*g.pl.*) 896⁷

þēh, *conj.* though 896¹⁴. See **þēah**

þēod, *f.ō-stem*, [THEDE] ; people, 867

þes, *dem.adj.* THIS ; **þisne**, *m.acc.sg.* 851 ; **þissum**, *d.sg.* 871²⁹, 889 ; **þysum** 892¹, 896¹ ; **þӯs**, *instr.sg.* 893¹, 894¹ ; **þisse**, *f.d.sg.* 885²⁷

þiderweardes, *adv.* THITHERWARDS, thither ; on his way there 893²⁹

þisse, see **þes**

þonces, *adv.* THANKS ; by the mercy 896⁴

þonne, *adv.* THEN 893⁶ ; *conj.* than 893¹⁸

þonon, *conj.* [THENNE] ; whence 891

þreo, see þrie

þridda, *adj.* THIRD ; *þ. fæder* great-grandfather 885²⁷ ; see healf

þrie, *num.adj.* THREE 891 ; þreo, *neut.* 895²² ; þrim, *dat.* 896⁵

þrītig, *adj.* THIRTY 878²⁶

þrōwian, *w.v.*(2), [THROW] ; suffer 885³⁶

geþungen, *p.pt.*(*as sb.*) distinguished ; *superl.* 896¹⁴

þurh, *prep.w.acc.* THROUGH 887¹

þus, *adv.* THUS 891

þūsend, *num.* THOUSAND 871²⁰

geþuærness, *f.jō-stem,* concord, peace, 860

þÿ, *conj.* because ; *þy . . . þy* therefore . . . because 836

þÿ, see sē

þyncan, *w.v.*(1b), *impers.w.dat.* [THINK] ; seem 896²³

þys(um), see þes

U

ufeweard, *adj.* higher, inner, 896²⁹

ufor, *adv.comp.* further up 881

under, *prep.* UNDER, under cover of, 865, 876

underfōn, *v.*(7), [UNDERFO] ; take, accept, 867

unēðelīce, see unieþelīce

ungecynd, *adj.* not of royal birth, low-born 867

ungemetlic, *adj.* immense 867

ungeþuærnes, *f.jō-stem,* discord, dissension, 867

unieþelīce, *adv.* with difficulty 878 , unēðelīce, awkwardly 896³⁵

unsibb, *f.jō-stem,* enmity, hostility, 887¹⁵

unwealt, *adj.* steady 896³¹

unwīs, *adj.* ·UNWISE, foolish 874

up, *adv.* UP 860

uppe, *adv.* up 896³⁰

ūt, *adv.* OUT 875

ūtan, *adv.* from without, outside, 893²⁷, &c ; without, to (on) the outside 885⁵, 896⁴⁷

ūte, *adv.* out 894⁹ ; outside 893¹⁸ ; out (on service) 893¹⁷

ūtermere, *m.i-stem,* outer waters, open sea, 896³⁸

ūteweard, *adj.* OUTWARD ; outer 892¹¹, 896³²

W

gewald, *m.a-stem,* [WIELD] ; power, control, command, 833 &c

gewalden, *adj.* small, inconsiderable 893⁴⁰n

gewægd, *p.pt.* distressed, troubled, 893⁸²

wæl, *n.a-stem,* [WAL] ; slaughter

wælsliht, *m.i-stem,* slaughter 839

wælstōw, *f. wō-stem,* place of slaughter, battlefield ; *ahton wælstowe gewald,* gained possession of the battlefield, won the battle, 833, &c

wæs, *p.t.sg.* WAS 838 ; was 853, &c ; remained 878¹⁷ ; wǣron, *pl.* 835n, wǣrun 855 ; wǣre, *subj.sg.* was, might be 893²⁰, should be 874

wæter, *n.a-stem,* WATER 896³⁸

wæter-fæsten, *n.ja-stem,* river-camp 893⁹

wē, *pron.* WE 851, 892²

weald, *m.u-stem,* WEALD, forest, 892¹⁰n

Wealhgerēfa, *m.n-stem,* the Welsh reeve 896⁵⁴*n

wel, *adv.* WELL ; much 893⁵⁷

welhwǽr, *adv.* almost everywhere 896²⁶

wendan, *w.v.(1b), often w.reflex.* WEND; turn, go, return, 885¹²

geweorc, *n.a-stem,* (military) WORK, encampment, 868, &c; **gewerc** 895¹⁶

weorpan, *v.(3),* [WARP]; cast 896⁴⁸

weorþan, *v.(3),* [WORTH]; be, become (*esp.w.p.pt.*) 833, &c

weorðian, *w.v.(2),* [WORTH]; honour 878³¹

weorþness, *f.jō-stem,* honour, dignity, 855

weorþust, *adj.superl.* most honourable 878²⁷

wered, *n.a-stem,* [WERED]; troop 871³⁵n

west, *adv.* WEST 876; **wæst,** in the west 893⁶⁶

westan, *adv.* from the west 893⁴²; *be westan,* on the west of, 893⁷⁴

west-dǽl, *m.i-stem,* western part 887¹³

wēste, *adj.* [WESTE]; deserted, desolate, 893⁹²n

westlang, *adv.* westwards, extending west 892⁷

west-rīce, *n.ja-stem,* western kingdom 885¹⁹

westweard, *adv.* WESTWARD 892²

wīc, *f.* or *n.* (*in pl.*) camp 878¹⁹

wica, see **wiece**

wīceng, *m.a-stem,* viking, 879

wīc-gerēfa, *m.n-stem,* townreeve, bailiff, 896¹³*

(ge)wīcian, *w.v.(2),* [WICK]; encamp, be encamped 893⁷

wiece, *f.n-stem,* WEEK 878²⁵; **wiecan,** *d.sg.* 878¹⁴; **wucena,** *g.pl.* 893⁸⁰; **wicum,** *d.pl.* 887⁶

wīf, *n.a-stem,* WIFE, woman, 893⁵³

winnan, *v.(3),* WIN; fight, struggle, 835, 878¹²

winter, *m.u-stem,* WINTER, year 833, 836, &c

winter-setl, *n.a-stem,* winterquarters 866

wiota, *m.n-stem* [WITE]; adviser, councillor 853

gewītan, *v.(1),* [WITE²]; turn, go, 885⁷

wiþ, *prep.w.acc.* WITH; against 837, 882, &c, (*after pron.*) 835, 851; *w.gen.* to, towards, 893³⁹; *w.dat.* with 865; against, in return for, 865; by, near 878²⁷

wolde, *p.t.* WOULD 877; *pl.* 874; wished, desired, 891, 893²⁰; (*subj.*) would wish to 874; would go 878¹³

gewrit, *n.a-stem,* [IWRIT]; letter 889

wucena, see **wiece**

wudu, *m.u-stem,* WOOD 892⁶

wudu-fæsten, *n.ja-stem,* the forest encampment 893⁹

gewundod, *p.pt.* wounded 893³¹

wunian, *w.v.(2),* [WONE]; dwell, remain, 855, 887¹¹

wyrcan, *w.v.(1b),* WORK; make, build, construct, 878, &c; **geworct,** *p.pt.* 893⁵⁰

Y

yfel, *n.a-stem,* EVIL, harm, 896²⁵

ymb, *prep.w.acc.* [UMBE]; about 855, 874; after 891; around 885³

ymbe, *prep.w.acc.* about 891, 892²

ymbsittan, *v.(5),* besiege, surround, 885³

ymbūtan, *adv.* about; *west y.* along the coast westward 877; 893³⁵

yst, *f.i-stem,* storm 877

70

INDEX OF PLACE-NAMES

Printed and bound by CPI Group (UK) Ltd, Croydon, CR0 4YY

14/04/2025

14656899-0001